KEFALC

THE UPDATED TRAVEL GUIDE

Discovering Kefalonia: From Mythical Caves to Beaches, Culture, and Ancient Wonders

John Schnell

TABLE OF CONTENTS

TABLE OF CONTENTS 3

INTRODUCTION 7

WELCOME TO KEFALONIA 11

Location and Geography 11

History 13

Culture and People 17

Weather and Climate 20

REASONS WHY YOU SHOULD VISIT KEFALONIA 23

SOME INTERESTING THINGS YOU PROBABLY DO
NOT KNOW ABOUT KEFALONIA 27

VISA REQUIREMENTS 31

THE BEST TIME TO VISIT 34

CULTURAL ETIQUETTE AND CUSTOMS 37

SOME USEFUL PHRASES AND VOCABULARY 43

Greetings and Basic Expressions 43

Basic Conversational Phrases 44

Ordering Food and Drinks: 44

Directions and Transportation 44

Basic Numbers 45

GETTING TO KEFALONIA 46

TRAVELING AROUND KEFALONIA 50

COST OF A TRIP TO KEFALONIA 56

MONEY-SAVING TIPS FOR BUDGET TRAVELERS 61

THINGS TO BRING ON A TRIP 69

HEALTH AND SAFETY ADVICE 74

POPULAR SCAMS TO BE AWARE OF 81

POPULAR ATTRACTIONS IN KEFALONIA 86

Myrtos Beach 86

Melissani Cave 89

Assos Village 91

Fiskardo 94

Skala Beach 97

Mount Ainos National Park 99

Argostoli 102

Assos Castle 105

Lighthouse of Saint Theodoroi 108

Saint Gerasimos Monastery 111

OFF-THE-BEATEN-PATH DESTINATIONS 115

OUTDOOR ACTIVITIES AND EXPERIENCES......... 119

NEARBY DAY TRIPS FROM KEFALONIA 124

A PERFECT SEVEN-DAY ITINERARY FOR A VISIT TO KEFALONIA... 130

Day 1: Arrival in Argostoli and City Exploration 130

Day 2: Myrtos Beach and Assos Village 131

Day 3: Melissani Cave and Fiskardo 131

Day 4: Boat Trip to Ithaca 132

Day 5: Beach-Hopping and Sea Kayaking 133

Day 6: Mount Ainos and Robola Wine Tasting.......... 133

Day 7: Lighthouse of Saint Theodoroi and Lassi Beach
.... 134

CULTURAL FESTIVALS AND HOLIDAYS 136

BEST BEACHES IN KEFALONIA 143

KEFALONIA FOR FAMILIES 147

Practical Tips and Recommendations for Traveling with Kids.. 151

KEFALONIA FOR COUPLES 156

KEFALONIA FOR ADVENTURE SEEKERS 164

SHOPPING AND DINING 169

Shopping 169

Dining 177

Some Dishes You Should Try When You Visit Kefalonia
.... 181

NIGHTLIFE IN KEFALONIA....................................... 186

ACCOMMODATION OPTIONS IN KEFALONIA 191

BEST TRAVEL RESOURCES 198

CONCLUSION.. 200

INTRODUCTION

As I stepped off the plane onto the sun-kissed tarmac, a warm breeze greeted me, instantly putting a smile on my face. I had arrived on the beautiful Greek island of Kefalonia, a place I had dreamed of visiting for years. The azure waters of the Ionian Sea sparkled in the distance, promising adventure and relaxation in equal measure.

I made my way to the hotel, a charming villa nestled on a hillside overlooking the picturesque town of Argostoli. The sight from my balcony was absolutely stunning. The pastel-colored buildings lined the harbor, and the rhythmic sound of boats gently bobbing in the water created a serene atmosphere.

Eager to explore, I ventured into the heart of the town. The streets were narrow and winding, adorned with vibrant flowers cascading from balconies and bougainvillea climbing the walls. The aroma of freshly baked pastries wafted through the air, luring me into a local bakery. I couldn't resist indulging in a mouthwatering spanakopita, a traditional Greek spinach and feta pastry.

Wandering along the waterfront, I came across a bustling fish market. Fishermen proudly displayed their catches of the day, an array of shimmering seafood that made my mouth water. I watched as locals and tourists haggled over the freshest fish, their conversations filled with lively gestures and laughter.

I decided to take a boat tour around the island, eager to discover the hidden gems of Kefalonia. The boat glided across the crystal-clear waters, revealing secluded coves and pristine beaches that looked like they belonged in a postcard. The captain regaled us with tales of the island's rich history, including its role in the Greek War of Independence and its prominence in Greek mythology.

One of the highlights of my trip was a visit to the iconic Myrtos Beach. Nestled between towering cliffs, the beach boasted a stunning combination of turquoise waters and powdery white sand. I couldn't resist the temptation to take a refreshing dip in the sea, the cool water washing away the cares of everyday life.

As the sun began to set, I found myself at the quaint village of Assos. Its charming Venetian-style houses clung to the hillside, creating a picturesque setting that felt like stepping back in time. I savored a delicious meal at a local taverna, indulging in traditional Greek delicacies such as moussaka and grilled octopus. The meal was accompanied by the melodious sounds of live bouzouki music, transporting me to a world of enchantment.

Throughout my visit, the warmth and hospitality of the locals left an indelible impression on me. Whether it was the shopkeeper who patiently helped me decipher Greek phrases or the friendly bartender who shared stories of island life, their genuine kindness made me feel like a welcomed guest rather than a tourist.

Leaving Kefalonia was bittersweet, as I had fallen in love with its natural beauty, rich history, and warm-hearted people. As I boarded the plane back home, I carried with me memories of sunsets over the Ionian Sea, the taste of olive oil on my lips, and the feeling of utter tranquility that only Kefalonia could offer. I vowed to return one day, to once again immerse myself in the magic of this Greek paradise.

WELCOME TO
KEFALONIA

Location and Geography

Kefalonia, also known as Cephalonia, is a beautiful Greek island off the western coast of mainland Greece in the Ionian Sea. It is the biggest of the Ionian Islands, with a varied terrain that includes the Rocky Mountains, lush woods, and stunning beaches.

Kefalonia is located around 50 kilometers west of the mainland city of Patras and has an area of approximately 780 square kilometers. It has an extended form that spans from northwest to southeast, with a length of around 50 kilometers and a maximum width of approximately 30 kilometers.

The island's geology is defined by its hilly topography, particularly the towering Mount Ainos, which rises at an astonishing 1,628 meters in height. Mount Ainos is a national park and a major part of the scenery of Kefalonia. Its slopes are densely forested, with the uncommon Abies cephalonica, a kind of fir tree found only on the island, dominating.

Kefalonia has a magnificent coastline that stretches for over 250 kilometers, in addition to its hilly parts. The island is known for its stunning beaches, which range from quiet coves to long lengths of sand. With its turquoise seas and magnificent rocks, Myrtos Beach on the northwest coast is possibly the most renowned of them all.

Argostoli, the island's capital and main town, is located on the island's western shore. With its picturesque waterfront promenade dotted with cafés, shops, and restaurants, the town overlooks a natural harbor and serves as a center of activity. Other prominent cities and villages on the island include Lixouri, Sami, and Fiskardo, each with its own distinct charm and personality.

Kefalonia is also famous for its geological structures like as caverns and subterranean lakes. The Melissani Cave, which is located near Sami, is a renowned tourist destination. Its partly collapsed ceiling has formed a stunning subterranean lake into which sunlight penetrates, generating captivating blue and green colors.

The island has a Mediterranean climate, with hot, dry summers and warm, rainy winters. Summer months, from June through September, are the busiest for tourists, with highs of roughly 30 degrees Celsius (86 degrees Fahrenheit). The seasons of spring and fall are mild, making them excellent for enjoying the island's natural beauties without the crowds.

History

Kefalonia's history, also known as Cephalonia's, is a rich tapestry that spans millennia. Kefalonia, located on the Ionian Sea off Greece's western coast, has been inhabited since ancient times and has seen the rise and fall of different civilizations throughout history.

The oldest evidence of human existence on Kefalonia goes back to the Paleolithic era, with archaeological discoveries indicating that the island was populated as early as 50,000 years ago. Farming populations appeared on the island at approximately 4000 BCE, leaving behind evidence of their dwellings and burial sites. These early colonists practiced fishing and hunting as well as developing a primitive kind of agriculture.

Kefalonia, like the rest of the Ionian Islands, was settled by the Greeks during the ancient Greek era. Because of its strategic position, it became a significant center of trade and business. The Cephalonians, a people said to be of Greek heritage, lived on the island.

Kefalonia thrived under the rule of many Greek city-states, including Corinth, Athens, and Sparta. The island became well-known for its winemaking, shipbuilding, and involvement in the Peloponnesian War between Athens and Sparta. Kefalonia supported Athens, and its strategic location made it a target for opposing powers.

After the Roman Republic conquered Greece in the second century BCE, Kefalonia fell under Roman authority. During this time, the island prospered economically, and Roman norms and traditions affected its society and culture.

Kefalonia, like the rest of Greece, came under Byzantine authority when the Western Roman Empire declined. During the Byzantine period, Christianity flourished over the island, with the building of several churches and monasteries. Under Byzantine administration, Kefalonia had a period of relative peace and prosperity that lasted until the entry of other powers in the Middle Ages.

The Venetian Dominion during the Medieval Period: Throughout the Middle Ages, Kefalonia was subjected to several invasions and occupations by different nations. The island fell under the influence of the Republic of Venice in the 13th century, which created a feudal system with local lords reigning over the island's sections. Kefalonia was significantly influenced culturally and architecturally during the Venetian era. Many fortresses, castles, and palaces were built, and many of them still survive today.

Ottoman and British Rule: The Ottomans seized Kefalonia in 1479, and the island remained under Ottoman control for over four centuries. The Cephalonians, on the other hand, wer`   e often involved in piracy in order to fight Ottoman domination. The strategic position of the island made it a target for different European nations vying for control of the eastern Mediterranean.

The Treaty of Campo Formio, signed in the late 18th century, ceded Kefalonia to the French Republic, commanded by Napoleon Bonaparte. During the Napoleonic Wars, however, the British took possession of the Ionian Islands, including Kefalonia, in 1809. The islands were under British authority until 1864, when they were reunited with Greece.

Kefalonia saw economic expansion and development with the integration of the Ionian Islands into Greece. However, the island was heavily damaged during World War II. It had been brutally bombarded, and many historical structures had been damaged or destroyed. During the war, Kefalonia played a part in the Greek resistance against Axis troops.

Kefalonia has been rebuilt and has become a renowned tourist resort after the war. Its natural splendor, attractive towns, and beautiful beaches draw tourists from all over the globe.

Today, Kefalonia flourishes as a dynamic component of contemporary Greece, honoring its rich heritage while seizing new chances. It is still an island of cultural history, beautiful scenery, and kind people.

Culture and People

Kefalonia's culture and people are strongly anchored in the island's long and diverse history. Kefalonia's cultural fabric is a remarkable combination of traditions, customs, and way of life, influenced by ancient Greek, Roman, Byzantine, Venetian, and British cultures.

The Cephalonians, the people of Kefalonia, are noted for their friendliness and hospitality. Hospitality is a fundamental part of their culture, and guests are often welcomed with open arms. Locals are proud to share their rich history, customs, and tales with visitors.

Music and dancing are important parts of Kefalonia's cultural life. Traditional folk music may be heard at festivals, weddings, and other events, and is often accompanied by instruments such as the mandolin, guitar, and violin. The island has its own distinct dance form, known as "Kefalonitiko," which is distinguished by vibrant motions and precise footwork.

Cephalonians put a high value on religion, with the majority of the people practicing Greek Orthodox Christianity. Throughout the island, there are several churches and monasteries, each with its unique history and religious importance. Religious festivals and pilgrimages are an important element of the cultural calendar because they bring communities together to celebrate their religion.

Kefalonia's food is a wonderful reflection of its history and environment. Fresh fish, locally produced vegetables, olive oil, and herbs are common ingredients in traditional recipes. The island is famed for its distinctive cheese, "kefalograviera," as well as its famous meat pie, "kreatopita." Winemaking has a long history in Kefalonia, with the Robola grape variety being particularly well-known.

The architecture of Kefalonia reflects the influence of numerous cultures throughout history. Venetian-style buildings may be found throughout the island's principal cities, such as Argostoli and Fiskardo, and are distinguished by their arched windows, wooden balconies, and colorful façade. Traditional stone buildings and villages with narrow walkways and flower-filled courtyards provide an insight into the island's bucolic history.

Festivals and cultural events are highly valued by the inhabitants of Kefalonia. The most renowned festival is the "Robola Wine Festival," which takes place in August and allows visitors to sample the island's famed wine while also enjoying traditional music and dance performances. Religious processions, carnivals, and music performances, for example, bring the community together and create a dynamic environment.

Kefalonia's natural beauty is also an important aspect of its cultural character. The island is known for its beautiful beaches, clean seas, and mountainous mountains. Exploring the caverns of the island, climbing through its mountains, and sailing along its shoreline are all popular activities that enable both inhabitants and tourists to interact with the island's natural environment.

Weather and Climate

Kefalonia has a Mediterranean climate with moderate winters and hot, dry summers. The weather on the island is affected by its position in the Ionian Sea, off Greece's western coast. Kefalonia's climate adds to its popularity as a tourist destination.

Summer (June to August): Kefalonia's summers are hot and dry, with lots of sunlight and little rain. During this season, average temperatures vary from 25 to 32 degrees Celsius (77 to 90 degrees Fahrenheit). It's peak tourist season, and the island is flooded with people looking to enjoy the lovely beaches and outdoor activities. During the summer, the sea temperature is pleasant and welcoming, ideal for swimming and water sports.

Autumn (September to November): Autumn in Kefalonia is marked by steadily falling temperatures and the occurrence of rain. With typical temperatures ranging from 20 to 27 degrees Celsius (68 to 81 degrees Fahrenheit) in September and gradually declining to 14 to 22 degrees Celsius (57 to 72 degrees Fahrenheit) in November, the weather stays pleasant and mild. Although tourism is less active at this time, visitors may still enjoy outdoor activities and discover the island's natural beauty.

Winter (December to February): Kefalonia's winters are moderate, but colder than the rest of the year. Temperatures average between 10 and 16 degrees Celsius (50 and 61 degrees Fahrenheit). While rainfall rises during this season, the island still receives plenty of sunlight. Winter is the quietest season on the island, making it suitable for anyone wanting a tranquil and undisturbed escape.

Spring (March to May): With flowering flowers and lush green surroundings, spring provides a rush of color and vitality to Kefalonia. In March, typical temperatures range from 13 to 19 degrees Celsius (55 to 66 degrees Fahrenheit) and gradually rise to 18 to 24 degrees Celsius (64 to 75 degrees Fahrenheit) in May. Spring is a great time to explore the island's nature paths, participate in outdoor activities, and see the island come alive after the winter months.

It's crucial to remember that weather patterns may change from year to year and that heat waves and storms can occur at any time of year. Before embarking on any outside activities or trips, it is prudent to consult the local weather forecast.

REASONS WHY YOU SHOULD VISIT KEFALONIA

Beautiful Beaches: Kefalonia has some of the most beautiful beaches in Greece. The island provides a range of coastal sceneries to discover and enjoy, from the famed Myrtos Beach with its turquoise waves and spectacular cliffs to the hidden beauty of Antisamos Beach.

Natural Beauty: The island is rich in natural beauty, with lush green mountains, intriguing caverns, and attractive vistas. The Melissani Cave and the Drogarati Cave are renowned tourist destinations that highlight the island's natural features.

Beautiful Drives: Kefalonia's meandering roadways provide beautiful drives that highlight the island's breathtaking landscapes. The trip from Argostoli to Assos, with its panoramic views of the coastline, and the drive from Sami to Poros, which passes through picturesque towns and olive orchards, are both remarkable experiences.

Kefalonia is rich in history and culture, and there are countless historical monuments and places to visit. Just a few examples of the island's remarkable legacy are the Venetian Castle of Assos, the Saint Gerasimos Monastery, and the Ancient Acropolis of Sami.

Culinary Delights: Foodies will enjoy the island's cuisine. Fresh fish, locally made olive oil, feta cheese, and traditional foods like moussaka and souvlaki will satisfy your palate. Don't forget to taste the local Robola wine, which is known for its distinct flavor.

Outdoor Activities: Kefalonia has a variety of outdoor activities for anyone looking for an adventure. There are several possibilities for satisfying your sense of adventure, ranging from hiking paths that lead you through breathtaking scenery to water activities like snorkeling, diving, and kayaking.

Kefalonia is home to a varied range of **wildlife and marine life**. Wild horses roam the island's woodlands, while sea turtles, dolphins, and seals may be seen in the surrounding seas. Nature enthusiasts will welcome the chance to see and admire these rare species.

Kefalonia is peppered with **picturesque villages** that provide an insight into the island's traditional way of life. Assos, Fiskardo, and Agia Efimia are well-known for their colorful buildings, tiny alleyways, and inviting ambiance, where you can enjoy authentic Greek hospitality.

Events: Throughout the year, the island holds a variety of events that allow you to immerse yourself in the local culture. The Robola Wine Festival, Saint Gerasimos' Feast, and Carnival festivities are just a few of the vibrant events that exhibit Kefalonia's traditions and customs.

Rest & Tranquility: While Kefalonia has many activities and attractions to offer, it also offers a calm and tranquil setting for people seeking rest. The tranquil environment, along with the natural beauty of the island, makes it a great place for relaxing and revitalizing the mind and body.

SOME INTERESTING THINGS YOU PROBABLY DO NOT KNOW ABOUT KEFALONIA

Kefalonia is the **biggest of the Ionian Islands**, with an area of around 781 square kilometers (302 square miles). Because of its vastness, it can support a wide diversity of scenery, from mountains and valleys to gorgeous coasts.

Kefalonia is home to **one of the world's most unusual geological occurrences,** the Katavothres Sinkholes. These sinkholes are noted for their unusual water flow and are found near Argostoli. Water enters the sinkholes and goes below, only to reappear 14 kilometers (8.7 miles) distant in the Melissani Cave.

Famous Beaches in Hollywood Films: The enthralling beauty of Kefalonia's beaches has captivated filmmakers. Myrtos Beach on the island was featured in the film "Captain Corelli's Mandolin," starring Nicolas Cage and Penélope Cruz, giving worldwide attention to this breathtaking site.

Residence to Caretta Caretta Turtles: The beaches of Kefalonia are home to the endangered loggerhead sea turtles known as Caretta Caretta. With protected places where these turtles may safely lay their eggs and hatch, the island plays an important role in their conservation efforts.

Kefalonia has a long history of **seismic activity**, with the most catastrophic earthquake happening in 1953. This earthquake destroyed the majority of the island's structures, having a huge influence on the island's architecture and urban development.

Kefalonia is well-known for its distinctive **vineyards and wine production.** Robola wine from the island is highly appreciated and has been designated as a Protected Designation of Origin (PDO). The hilly topography and mineral-rich soil contribute to the grapes' distinct taste.

Odysseus and Mythology: Kefalonia is said to be the fabled home of Odysseus, the protagonist of Homer's epic poem "The Odyssey." Elements of the renowned story are thought to have been inspired by the island's craggy shoreline and caverns, such as the Melissani Cave.

Argostoli's Vivid Wildlife: Argostoli, the capital city of Kefalonia, is noted for its vivid wildlife. The nearby Koutavos Lagoon is home to a variety of bird species, including herons and black-headed gulls. Birdwatchers may have a great view from the lagoon's bridge.

Melissani Underground Lake: The Melissani Cave, near Sami, has a fascinating underground lake. Sunlight flowing through a hole in the caves top illuminates the crystal-clear turquoise waters, providing visitors with a bizarre and mesmerizing experience.

Kefalonia is filled with **charming and aristocratic villages** that radiate charm and character. Tourists go to Fiskardo, noted for its colorful Venetian-style houses, while Assos, nestled on a peninsula, provides stunning views of the Ionian Sea.

These intriguing facts show Kefalonia's distinctiveness and attractiveness. The island has plenty to offer anyone looking for a unique holiday experience, from its geological marvels and cinematic beaches to its cultural legacy and natural beauty.

VISA REQUIREMENTS

Kefalonia is an island in Greece, and as such, it is subject to the same visa requirements as the rest of the country. Most nationals of countries outside the European Union (EU) will need to obtain a visa in order to enter Kefalonia.

There are a few exceptions, however, such as nationals of the United States, Canada, Australia, and New Zealand, who can enter Kefalonia without a visa for up to 90 days.

If you are a national of a country that requires a visa to enter Kefalonia, you can obtain one from the nearest Greek embassy or consulate. The process for obtaining a visa varies depending on your nationality, but generally speaking, you will need to provide your passport, a recent photograph, and a completed visa application form. You may also be required to provide proof of travel arrangements, such as a plane ticket or hotel reservation.

The cost of a visa for Kefalonia varies depending on your nationality. Nationals of the United States, Canada, Australia, and New Zealand can obtain a visa for €20. Nationals of other countries may be required to pay a higher fee.

Once you have obtained a visa, you will be able to enter Kefalonia for up to 90 days. If you wish to stay in Kefalonia for longer than 90 days, you will need to apply for a residence permit.

Here are the specific visa requirements for some of the most common nationalities:

United States: Nationals of the United States do not need a visa to enter Kefalonia for up to 90 days.

Canada: Nationals of Canada do not need a visa to enter Kefalonia for up to 90 days.

Australia: Nationals of Australia do not need a visa to enter Kefalonia for up to 90 days.

New Zealand: Nationals of New Zealand do not need a visa to enter Kefalonia for up to 90 days.

United Kingdom: Nationals of the United Kingdom need a visa to enter Kefalonia. A visa will set you back €60.

European Union: Nationals of EU countries do not need a visa to enter Kefalonia.

You can get more updated information here https://www.mfa.gr/en/visas/visas-for-foreigners-traveling-to-greece/

THE BEST TIME TO VISIT

The ideal time to visit Kefalonia is determined by your interests and the sort of experience you desire. The climate on the island is Mediterranean, with warm winters and hot, dry summers. Here is a list of the seasons and what they have to offer:

Summer (June to August): Due to the hot and sunny weather, summer is the busiest tourist season in Kefalonia. Temperatures typically vary from 25 and 32 degrees Celsius (77 and 90 degrees Fahrenheit), making it excellent for beach activities and water sports. The water is warm and welcoming, making swimming and snorkeling ideal. However, keep in mind that summer may be rather congested, particularly in major tourist destinations. Summer is the greatest time to come if you love a bustling environment, and active nightlife, and appreciate the rush of the peak season.

Spring (March to May) and fall (September to November): Spring and fall are considered

Kefalonia's shoulder seasons, with good weather and fewer tourists. Temperatures vary from 13 to 27 degrees Celsius (55 to 81 degrees Fahrenheit) throughout these months, making it ideal for outdoor activities like as hiking, touring towns, and sightseeing.

Spring gives blossoming flowers and lush green landscapes, whilst autumn brings warm temperatures and light rain. These seasons are great for individuals looking for a mix of good weather, fewer visitors, and the chance to explore the island's natural beauties.

Winter (December to February): Kefalonia's winters are moderate, but colder than the rest of the year. Temperatures average between 10 and 16 degrees Celsius (50 and 61 degrees Fahrenheit). Even though winter is the off-season, the island nonetheless provides a tranquil and serene setting. It's a great opportunity to learn about the local way of life, see historical places, and spend quiet nights in tavernas. It is crucial to remember, however, that certain tourist attractions may have restricted hours or be closed at this time.

It's worth noting that the weather in Kefalonia may change from year to year, with occasional heatwaves or storms occurring at any time of year. If you plan on doing any outside activities, such as hiking or water sports, you should examine the weather conditions during your selected vacation date.

CULTURAL ETIQUETTE AND CUSTOMS

Greeks are typically warm and cordial, and greetings are a significant aspect of social contact. It is usual to extend a handshake and keep eye contact while greeting someone. In more formal circumstances, using "Mr." (Kyrios) or "Mrs." (Kyria) followed by the person's last name is a respectful approach to addressing someone.

Punctuality: Being fashionably late is more frequent in Greek society. Arriving a few minutes beyond the agreed-upon time is appropriate for social gatherings or activities. However, it is still preferable to be on time for business meetings and formal functions.

Respect for Religion: Greece, especially Kefalonia, has a rich religious legacy, with Greek Orthodox Christians being the majority of the population. It is vital to dress modestly and properly while visiting churches or monasteries. Women should cover their shoulders and refrain from wearing shorts or exposing apparel, while males should refrain from wearing caps.

Dining Etiquette: Greeks take their meals seriously and see them as a social occasion to be shared with friends and family. It is usual to provide a little gift for the host, such as flowers or a bottle of wine when welcomed to a Greek house. Because Greeks like to share their meal, it is customary to see a variety of dishes arranged in the middle of the table for everyone to enjoy. It is customary to sample a little bit of everything and to never leave food on your plate. Also, bear in mind that Greeks prefer to eat slowly, so give plenty of time to savor the meal and participate in the conversation.

Tipping is valued but not required in Greece. If the service was acceptable, it is customary to leave a little tip of 5-10% of the total. Rounding up the tab or leaving loose change is a common practice at cafés and bars. It's usually a good idea to double-check the statement to see whether a service fee has already been included.

Greeks are expressive and often utilize hand gestures and body language to enhance their remarks. However, some gestures, such as creating an "O" shape with your hand or employing the palm-upward "OK" sign, may be deemed insulting in Greece. To avoid misunderstandings, it's advisable to avoid employing these gestures.

While Kefalonia is a major tourist destination, it is nevertheless appropriate to **dress modestly**, particularly while visiting religious sites or more conservative communities. It is advised that you wear clothes that cover your shoulders and knees. Swimwear is permissible on the beaches, although it is polite to cover up while leaving the beach area.

Public Behavior: Greeks value courtesy and care for others. In public areas, loud or disruptive conduct is often frowned upon. Remember that smoking is not permitted in any interior public location, including restaurants and cafés.

While English is widely spoken in many tourist destinations, travelers who make an effort to acquire a few basic Greek words are usually welcomed. Simple pleasantries such as "hello" (yassas) and "thank you" (efharisto) may go a long way toward establishing respect and a good relationship with the people.

Plate Breaking: While plate-breaking is often connected with Greek culture, it is not a frequent practice in Kefalonia or much of Greece nowadays. It is more of a stereotype that may be noticed in particular performances or on special occasions. So, although it is amusing to see, it is not a common practice in regular life.

Personal Space & Physical Contact: Greeks are typically warm and pleasant, and during talks, they may engage in greater physical contact, such as small taps on the arm or back. Personal space may be tighter than you are used to, particularly when interacting with friends or family. It is critical to maintain personal limits while still being receptive to cultural differences in physical touch.

Siesta Time: The Greek way of life, like many other Mediterranean civilizations, incorporates a siesta or noon nap. You may notice a slower pace and some companies shutting for a few hours in the afternoon, particularly in smaller towns or villages. Locals use this time to unwind, eat a leisurely lunch, or just rest. It is a part of the local rhythm of life and is best enjoyed by adopting a more relaxed attitude during these hours.

"Filoxenia" (Hospitality): Greeks are renowned for their warm hospitality, and the concept of "filoxenia" is deeply ingrained in their culture. Visitors to Kefalonia may expect to be greeted warmly and with real kindness by the inhabitants. It is customary for Greeks to serve food or beverages to visitors in order to make them feel at ease. Accept this hospitality with appreciation and return the favor whenever feasible.

Traditional Festivals and Traditions: Throughout the year, Kefalonia, like the rest of Greece, celebrates a variety of traditional festivals and traditions. These gatherings often include music, dancing, and eating.

If you have the chance to attend such festivals, it is a terrific way to immerse yourself in the local culture and celebratory mood.

Kefalonia is rich in history and historical landmarks, including castles, monasteries, and archaeological remains. It is important **to respect the historical value and cultural legacy** of these sites while visiting them. Respect any regulations or instructions that are offered, avoid littering, and avoid touching or harming any objects or buildings.

Visitors may develop meaningful relationships, have great interactions with residents, and really enjoy Kefalonia's distinct cultural history by being aware of and respecting the island's cultural etiquette and traditions. It is always best to approach your vacation with an open mind, accepting local traditions, and eager to learn from the rich cultural tapestry that Kefalonia has to offer.

SOME USEFUL PHRASES AND VOCABULARY

When visiting Kefalonia, it can be helpful to familiarize yourself with some basic Greek phrases and vocabulary. While many people in tourist areas speak English, knowing a few keywords and expressions can enhance your travel experience and show appreciation for the local culture. Check out these helpful expressions to get a better grasp of things:

Greetings and Basic Expressions:

Hello: (Yassas)

Good morning: (Kalimera)

Good evening: (Kalispera)

Goodbye: (Adio)

Please: (Parakalo)

Thank you: (Efharisto)

You're welcome: (Parakalo)

Yes: (Ne)

No: (Ohi)

Basic Conversational Phrases:

Do you speak English?: (Milate Agglika?)

I don't understand: (Den katalaveno)

Excuse me: (Sygnomi)

Sorry: (Lypamai)

Can you help me?: (Borite na me voithisete?)

Where is...?: (Pou ine...?)

How much does it cost?: (Poso kostizi?)

Ordering Food and Drinks:

I would like...: (Tha ithela...)

A table for two, please: (Ena trapezi gia dio, parakalo)

What do you recommend?: (Ti protinete?)

The bill, please: (To logariasmo, parakalo)

Cheers!: (Ygeia!)

Directions and Transportation:

Where is the nearest...?: (Pou ine to plisiestero...?)

Can you call a taxi for me?: (Borite na mou kalesete ena taxi?)

Where is the bus station?: (Pou ine i stasi tou leoforeiou?)

Is it far?: (Ine makria?)

Left: (Aristera)

Right: (Dexia)

Straight ahead: (Katefthian)

Basic Numbers:

One: (Ena)

Two: (Dio)

Three: (Tria)

Four: (Tessera)

Five: (Pente)

Ten: (Deka)

Twenty: (Ikosi)

Hundred: (Ekato)

Thousand: (Hilia)

Remember, locals will appreciate your efforts to speak some Greek, even if it's just a few basic phrases. It can help you navigate the island, connect with the people, and create memorable experiences during your visit to Kefalonia.

GETTING TO KEFALONIA

Kefalonia is reasonably simple to reach, with various transportation choices available. The following are the major methods to get to the island:

By Air:

Flying is the most convenient method to travel to Kefalonia. Kefalonia International Airport "Anna Pollatou," often known as EFL, is the island's international airport. The airport is situated in the Svoronata district, some 8 kilometers (5 miles) south of Argostoli, Kefalonia's city.

During the peak tourist season (April to October), many airlines provide direct flights to Kefalonia from major European cities. Aegean Airlines, Ryanair, and easyJet are among the airlines that service the airport. You may easily reach your hotel from the airport via taxi, private transport, or rental vehicle.

By Ferry:

Another frequent mode of transportation to Kefalonia is by ferry. There are several ferry connections from Greece's mainland and other surrounding islands. Kefalonia's major ferry ports are Poros, Sami, and Argostoli. Ferry services are available from a number of mainland ports, including Patras and Kyllini, as well as surrounding islands like Zakynthos and Lefkada.

The ferry voyage time varies based on the route and kind of vessel, ranging from a few hours to several hours. Ionian Ferries and Kefalonian Lines are two ferry companies that serve Kefalonia. Check the timetables and purchase your tickets ahead of time, particularly during high season.

By Road:

If you prefer to travel by car, you may reach Kefalonia from different areas of Greece. A bridge that spans the Gulf of Corinth connects the island to the mainland. You may drive to Patras from Athens, take the ferry to Sami or Poros in Kefalonia, and then continue your trip by road. The journey from Patras to Sami takes around 3-4 hours, not counting the ferry crossing.

The island's road network is typically in excellent shape, enabling you to explore various places at your leisure. Rental cars are accessible at the airport, ferry terminals, and major cities.

By Bus:

The primary bus operator in Kefalonia is KTEL, which provides bus services to numerous places on the island. Major cities such as Argostoli, Sami, and Lixouri, as well as various villages and beaches, are served by buses.

If you already have a Greek passport, you may take a bus from Athens to Patras and then transfer to a boat to Kefalonia. The bus ride from Athens to Patras takes around three hours.

It's important to note that transportation schedules and frequencies may change depending on the season, so check the schedules and make any required bookings ahead of time, particularly during the high summer months. Furthermore, if you are visiting from a country other than Greece, you should verify visa regulations and other essential travel papers before organizing your trip.

TRAVELING AROUND KEFALONIA

Kefalonia has various simple transit choices for travelers to experience the island's gorgeous scenery, quaint towns, and breathtaking beaches. Here are several options for getting about Kefalonia:

Renting a vehicle is a popular way to explore Kefalonia independently and at your own leisure. Car rental companies may be located at the airport, major cities, and prominent tourist destinations. Having a vehicle allows you to go to isolated beaches, attractive towns, and stunning vistas.

The island's road network is typically well-kept, albeit certain hilly locations may have small and twisting roadways. Keep in mind that driving in Greece is done on the right side of the road. It's best to reserve your rental vehicle ahead of time, particularly during the high tourist season.

Taxis: Taxis are widely accessible in Kefalonia and provide an easy means to commute between cities, villages, and important tourist destinations. Taxis are available at taxi ranks, airports, ferry terminals, and significant squares.

It is best to negotiate the fee with the driver before beginning the ride or to confirm that the taxi is equipped with a meter. Taxis may also be booked for half-day or full-day trips to visit the island's many sites.

Local Buses: KTEL operates a dependable and reasonably priced bus network that links major cities, villages, and tourist beaches in Kefalonia. Buses are a cheap way to get across the island, particularly for shorter distances. The primary bus station is in Argostoli, and buses go to many places on a regular basis. Timetables and routes may change according to the season, therefore it's best to double-check the timetables ahead of time. Tickets may be bought from the bus driver or at the bus terminal.

Boats & Ferries: The coastline of Kefalonia is filled with gorgeous beaches and secret bays, and one of the finest ways to discover these treasures is by boat.

Several businesses provide boat trips, cruises, and water taxis, allowing visitors to explore quiet beaches, sea caves, and adjacent islands like Ithaca and Zakynthos. Additionally, frequent ferry routes link Kefalonia to other Greek islands and the mainland, enabling you to go island hopping or take day excursions to surrounding sites.

Scooters and All-Terrain Vehicles (ATVs): For a fun and exciting way to navigate about Kefalonia, try hiring a scooter or an all-terrain vehicle (ATV). ATVs and scooters are perfect for exploring tight hamlet streets and getting to smaller beaches. They are available for hire at numerous sites across the island, and most need a valid driver's license.

Walking and Cycling: Kefalonia has great natural beauty, and exploring the island on foot or by bicycle is a terrific opportunity to get a close-up look at its charm. You may go for a leisurely stroll along the shore, trek along magnificent trails, or bike through lovely towns. There are many planned walking tours and cycling routes available to suit a variety of interests and fitness levels.

Organized Tours & Excursions: If you prefer a guided experience, Kefalonia offers a variety of organized tours and excursions. Boat vacations, island tours, wine-tasting sessions, and cultural excursions are examples of these. When you join a guided tour, you can sit back, relax, and let professional guides show you the finest of Kefalonia.

Bicycle Rentals: For those who prefer riding, renting a bicycle is an excellent way to discover the stunning landscapes of Kefalonia. Many rental businesses provide bicycles for varying lengths of time, enabling you to peddle along seaside routes, explore the countryside, or go through picturesque villages. Kefalonia's modest size and diversified topography make it ideal for both leisurely rides and more difficult routes.

Local Mini-Buses: In addition to conventional bus services, Kefalonia offers mini-buses that run along specialized routes, especially in attractive tourist locations. These mini-buses often link beaches, hotels, and significant attractions, making them a simple way to go about within a certain zone. They're particularly beneficial if you don't want to drive or are vacationing in a resort region with few transit choices.

Walking: The natural beauty and mild temperature of Kefalonia make it a perfect location for walkers and hikers. There are various trails and walkways that snake through gorgeous landscapes, providing an opportunity to find hidden treasures and take in spectacular vistas. Mount Ainos National Park, Melissani Cave to Karavomilos, and the seaside walk from Argostoli to Lassi are all popular hiking destinations. Bring appropriate footwear, drink, and verify the difficulty level of the paths before starting out.

Motorbike Rentals: If you've never ridden a motorcycle or scooter before, hiring one may be a handy and thrilling way to see Kefalonia. Motorcycles have more movement and agility, enabling you to cross tight streets and reach quiet areas that a vehicle would not be able to reach.

However, be sure you have the required license and follow all traffic laws and safety procedures.

Horseback Riding: Horseback riding is a unique and fascinating way to discover Kefalonia. On the island, many equestrian facilities provide guided riding trips via gorgeous paths and beaches. You may enjoy a leisurely ride, observe the island's natural beauty, and get a new perspective on Kefalonia's terrain whether you're a newbie or an experienced rider.

Kefalonia's small size and well-connected infrastructure make it simple to visit the island's natural treasures, historical attractions, and picturesque towns, regardless of the method of transportation. To choose the best choice for your Kefalonia journey, consider your preferences, timetable, and the desired amount of freedom.

COST OF A TRIP TO KEFALONIA

Flights to Kefalonia vary in price depending on your departure location, the time of year, and how far in advance you book. Flights are often more costly during the peak tourist season (April to October) than during the offseason. It's best to book your flights ahead of time to get the best rates.

Lodging: Kefalonia has a variety of lodging alternatives to suit all budgets. There are luxury resorts, boutique hotels, family-run guesthouses, self-catering flats, and budget-friendly options to pick from. Prices will vary according to location, amenities, and time of year. Accommodation expenses are often higher during the busy summer months, so travel during the shoulder or off-season to save money.

Meals & Eating: The price of meals in Kefalonia varies according to your eating choices. Eating at local tavernas, where you may sample traditional Greek food, is often less expensive than dining at upmarket places. There are also lots of self-catering choices if you want to make your meals with fresh local ingredients. A regular lunch out might cost anywhere from modest to expensive, depending on the establishment and the things you choose.

Renting a vehicle allows you to explore the island at your leisure, but you must consider rental fees, petrol expenditures, and parking taxes. Taxis are available, but the costs may add up quickly, particularly over longer distances. Local buses are a more cost-effective way to go about the island. Boat trips and excursions may have additional expenses based on the activities and places you choose.

Activities and Sightseeing: From beach hopping and seeing natural beauties to visiting historical sites and indulging in water sports, Kefalonia has something for everyone. The cost of these activities will vary according to your choices. You should budget for admission costs to attractions such as caverns, museums, and historical sites.

Souvenirs & Shopping: Keep in mind that costs might fluctuate if you want to buy souvenirs or go shopping. Popular gifts include local handicrafts, olive oil, honey, wine, and traditional items. Prices for these things might vary depending on their quality and where they are purchased.

Seasonal Variations: The cost of a vacation to Kefalonia might vary depending on the time of year you visit. The peak tourist season, which runs from June to August, is often the costliest in terms of lodging, airfare, and activities. Flight and hotel prices are often cheaper during the shoulder seasons of spring (April to May) and fall (September to October). Visiting during these periods might help you get better discounts and perhaps enjoy lower prices.

Travel Insurance: Travel insurance is strongly advised to protect yourself against unexpected occurrences such as trip cancellations, medical crises, or misplaced luggage. The cost of travel insurance varies according to the coverage and length of your trip. Compare many insurance companies and plans to get the one that best meets your requirements.

Currency & Exchange Rates: Greece's currency is the Euro (€). Check the exchange rates before your travel and consider exchanging money in advance for better prices. It's also a good idea to have extra cash on hand for smaller shops that may not take credit cards, particularly in rural locations.

Budgeting Tips: To efficiently control your costs, set a budget and monitor your spending throughout your vacation. Prepare by researching and comparing rates for lodging, airfare, and activities. To save money on eating, consider renting lodgings with self-catering amenities. Choose local restaurants and tavernas for traditional food at more reasonable costs. Look for special deals or reduced activity and trip packages.

Extra expenses to consider include airport transfers, visa fees (if required), and any extra services or facilities you may need during your stay. It's also a good idea to budget for any unforeseen costs or unplanned activities that may arise during your vacation.

Bargaining & Negotiating: While bargaining is not as popular in Kefalonian stores and restaurants, there may be some price flexibility at local markets or when buying bigger products or services. It's always worth respectfully asking if there's any opportunity for bargaining to get a better deal.

By taking these things into account and organizing your trip appropriately, you will be able to make more educated choices regarding your spending and have a better grasp of the total cost of your vacation to Kefalonia. To guarantee a memorable and pleasurable stay on this gorgeous Greek island, select the activities that are most important to you and manage your funds appropriately.

MONEY-SAVING TIPS FOR BUDGET TRAVELERS

If you're considering a low-cost vacation to Kefalonia, there are various money-saving techniques and methods that may help you get the most out of your trip without breaking the bank. Here are some ideas to think about:

Shoulder Season Travel: Consider visiting Kefalonia in the spring (April to May) or fall (September to October), when visitor crowds are less and rates for flights and lodgings are lower. You may still enjoy good weather and more unhurried exploration of the island.

Accommodation Options: Look for low-cost options including guesthouses, small hotels, or self-catering flats. When compared to luxury resorts, these choices often give minimal facilities at lower prices. Consider vacationing in smaller towns or villages distant from big tourist destinations, which may provide greater value.

Self-Catering: Save money on eating out by staying in a place that has a kitchen. You may create your meals by purchasing fresh produce, local items, and supplies from markets or supermarkets. This enables you to sample local delicacies, eat at your own speed, and save money on restaurant bills.

Local Eateries & Tavernas: When dining out, pick classic Greek tavernas and smaller family-owned eateries. In comparison to posh eateries, these outlets often provide ample quantities at moderate pricing. Look for daily specials or set meals that are reasonably priced.

Picnics & Beach Snacks: Picnics are a great way to enjoy Kefalonia's stunning scenery and beaches. Pack your own sandwiches, fruits, snacks, and beverages for a low-cost supper with a breathtaking view. There are several lovely areas where you may unwind and enjoy your home-cooked meal.

To travel about the island, take use **of low-cost transportation choices** like local buses or shared taxis. KTEL's public buses provide reasonable prices and link major cities and attractions. For short-distance exploration, consider hiring a bicycle or scooter, which may be less expensive than renting a vehicle.

Free and Low-Cost Activities: Kefalonia has a lot of natural beauty and attractions that don't cost a lot of money. Spend time exploring the island's beaches, hiking trails, and stunning overlooks, many of which are free. Visit public parks, museums, and churches with low or no admission costs. Take advantage of Kefalonia's natural beauty and outdoor activities without breaking the bank.

Schedule Your Activities Ahead of Time: Research and schedule your activities ahead of time to take advantage of any discounts or early bird prices. Some attractions and water sports establishments may offer discounted fees for online reservations or at specific times of the day. You may find better bargains and make the most of your money by preparing ahead of time.

Water Activities: Enjoy Kefalonia's gorgeous beaches and crystal-clear seas without breaking the bank. Pack your snorkeling equipment to explore the underwater marine life, hire a kayak or paddleboard for a fun and inexpensive trip, or just rest on the beach and soak up the rays.

Souvenir Shopping: If you want to purchase souvenirs, go to local markets or smaller businesses away from tourist traps. When compared to high-end boutiques or souvenir stores in prominent tourist locations, these establishments often offer more moderate pricing for traditional handicrafts, local items, and souvenirs.

While bargaining and negotiating are not as popular in established businesses and restaurants, you may practice your **negotiating abilities** at local markets or while buying bigger things or services. Ask politely whether there is any possibility of negotiating in order to achieve a better price.

Tap Water: Instead of buying bottled water, bring a reusable water bottle and fill it with Kefalonia's safe-to-drink tap water. In this manner, you may save money on bottled water while also reducing plastic waste.

Free Attractions and Events: Look for free attractions, events, and festivals throughout your vacation. Throughout the year, Kefalonia holds a variety of cultural events, concerts, and festivals, some of which are free to the public. Take advantage of these free chances to learn about and enjoy local culture, music, and customs.

Local Markets: Experience the colorful ambiance of local markets while discovering fresh vegetables, local items, and handicrafts. When opposed to tourist-oriented businesses, these marketplaces often provide a more genuine and economical buying experience. Fruits, vegetables, cheese, olives, and other regional delights may be purchased at moderate costs.

Consider Sharing Accommodation and Transportation Expenses: If you're traveling with a group or as a family, think about splitting lodging and transportation expenses. Renting a bigger apartment or villa and dividing the costs may be less expensive than renting numerous hotel rooms. Similarly, sharing a cab or auto rental with other people might help you save money.

Plan Your Meals Strategically: Take advantage of local eateries' lunchtime meals or "menu of the day" specials. for lunch hours, many restaurants offer cheap set menus that frequently contain a range of meals at a lesser price than ordering à la carte for supper. You may have a great supper without breaking the wallet this way.

Make Use of Free Services: Many Kefalonia lodgings include free services including breakfast, Wi-Fi, and access to swimming pools or recreational facilities. Take advantage of these goodies to save money on extra costs. Instead of paying for breakfast at a restaurant, take advantage of the complementary meal provided by your lodging.

Avoid Popular Tourist Sites: Prices in popular tourist sites in Kefalonia tend to be higher owing to increased demand. Consider visiting lesser-known cities, villages, and beaches where lodging, eating, and shopping may be more reasonable. Away from the masses, these regions typically give a more genuine and serene experience.

Stay Hydrated at the Beach: Purchasing refreshments at beach bars or kiosks may quickly add up. Bring your own reusable water bottle and refill it at public water fountains or beach showers to save money. Instead of buying pricey food, you may pack snacks and beverages from a store and have a picnic at the beach.

Special Offers & Discounts: Before your journey, look online for special offers, discounts, or travel passes that may be applicable to Kefalonia. When reserving in advance or as part of a package deal, several websites offer reduced pricing for lodgings, activities, or transportation. Look for coupons, promotional codes, or group discounts that will help you save money.

By following these money-saving ideas, you may enjoy a low-cost vacation to Kefalonia without sacrificing the island's beauty, experiences, and cuisines. Remember, it's all about prioritizing what's important to you and coming up with inventive methods to stretch your budget while visiting this lovely Greek vacation.

THINGS TO BRING ON A TRIP

When preparing for a vacation to Kefalonia, think about what you'll need for a comfortable and pleasurable stay on the island. Here are some specific recommendations about what to bring:

Pack lightweight, breathable clothes such as t-shirts, shorts, skirts, dresses, and lightweight trousers since Kefalonia has a Mediterranean environment with scorching summers. Don't forget to pack a couple of swimsuits for beach days.

Sun protection is essential in Kefalonia, particularly during the summer months. To protect your skin from the sun's rays, bring sunscreen with a high SPF, sunglasses, a wide-brimmed hat, and a lightweight scarf or cover-up.

Bring suitable walking shoes or sandals since you will most likely be doing a lot of walking and touring. Flip-flops or water shoes are ideal for the beach, while sturdy shoes or hiking boots are advised if you want to hike or explore nature paths.

Beach Essentials: With its beautiful beaches, you'll want to be ready to spend days by the water. Bring a beach towel, mat, or blanket, as well as a beach bag and a collapsible cooler for beverages and snacks. Remember to bring a reusable water bottle to remain hydrated.

When visiting the island, a compact **daypack or backpack** is ideal for carrying basics like as water, sunscreen, food, a camera, and other personal belongings.

Electrical Adapters: Because Greece utilizes Europlug (Type C) outlets, pack the essential adapters if your gadgets have various plug types.

Drugs and First Aid Kit: If you use prescription drugs, make sure you bring enough for the length of your vacation. It's also a good idea to include a basic first-aid kit, which should include bandages, antiseptic cream, painkillers, and any other personal prescriptions or supplies you may need.

Pack your passport, visa (if applicable), travel insurance paperwork, and any other necessary identity or travel documents. It's a good idea to preserve separate digital and physical copies of these papers for backup.

While internet resources are available, owning a **printed travel guide or map** of Kefalonia may be useful for exploring the island, learning about attractions, and uncovering hidden treasures.

Bring cash in Euros for little purchases, gratuities, and establishments that may not take cards. It's also a good idea to have a credit or debit card on hand for bigger purchases or emergencies. To prevent problems with overseas transactions, notify your bank or card issuer of your vacation intentions.

Waterproof Bag or Dry Bag: If you intend on participating in water sports or on a boat trip, a waterproof bag or dry bag may assist protect your gadgets, papers, and other valuables from water damage.

Insect Repellent: While Kefalonia does not have a large mosquito issue, having some insect repellent on hand is usually a good idea, particularly if you want to tour nature reserves or trek in forested regions.

Portable Charger and Travel Adapter: Bring a portable charger or power bank to keep your electronic gadgets charged when traveling. Furthermore, having a travel adaptor ensures that you may charge your gadgets using local power sources.

Snorkeling Equipment: If you like snorkeling, bring your own snorkel, mask, and fins to save money on rental fees. The clean seas off the coast of Kefalonia provide good prospects for underwater exploration.

Entertainment: Don't forget to bring your favorite form of downtime entertainment, such as books, e-readers, music, or games. It's wonderful to have something to look forward to during downtime or lengthy travels.

To avoid extra costs, remember to pack effectively and examine the airline's luggage regulations. Also, make room in your suitcase for any souvenirs or memories you may wish to bring back from Kefalonia.

HEALTH AND SAFETY ADVICE

When visiting Kefalonia, it is essential to prioritize your health and safety. Here are some specific health and safety recommendations for your trip:

Travel Insurance: Get comprehensive travel insurance that covers medical expenditures, trip cancellation, lost luggage, and emergency evacuation. Familiarize yourself with the policy's coverage and have the insurance information handy throughout your vacation.

Medical Preparations: Before flying, check with your doctor to make sure you're up to date on standard immunizations. It's also a good idea to ask about any recommended immunizations for Greece. Carry a sufficient supply of any prescription drugs you need, as well as a duplicate of your prescriptions.

Sun Protection: Kefalonia has a lot of sun, so protect yourself from damaging UV rays. Wear a wide-brimmed hat, sunglasses, and lightweight, long-sleeved clothes on a daily basis, as well as sunscreen with a high SPF. Seek cover during high solar hours (between 10 a.m. and 4 p.m.).

Stay Hydrated: Stay hydrated by drinking lots of water, particularly during the hot summer months. Carry a reusable water bottle and fill it with Kefalonia's safe-to-drink bottled or tap water.

Food and Water Safety: In general, Kefalonia has good food and water safety regulations. However, bottled water is recommended, particularly if you have a sensitive stomach. Consume fresh, properly cooked meals rather than uncooked or undercooked food. Wash your hands often, particularly before eating, to practice excellent hand hygiene.

Although Kefalonia does not have a large mosquito issue, it is prudent to protect yourself from bug bites. Wear **bug repellent**, particularly at night or while visiting forested regions. Consider wearing long-sleeved shirts and trousers, especially around twilight and early.

Emergency Services: Learn about emergency phone numbers in Greece. The universal emergency number is 112, which may be used to contact police, ambulances, or fire departments. Save vital phone numbers, such as those for your embassy or consulate, local hospitals, and emergency contact information for your lodging.

Road Safety: If you want to hire a vehicle or drive in Kefalonia, get acquainted with the local traffic laws and regulations. Wear your seatbelt at all times, obey speed limits, and avoid drinking and driving. Drive with caution on narrow and curving roads, particularly in rural regions.

Water Safety: Kefalonia has magnificent beaches, however, swimming should be done with care. Pay attention to warning signs, obey lifeguard directions, and be wary of strong currents or waves. Swim in approved locations and keep an eye out for any risks like pebbles or underwater currents.

Small Theft Avoidance: While Kefalonia is typically secure, take precautions to avoid small theft. Keep your valuables protected and be aware of your surroundings in busy places, public transit, and tourist attractions. When not in use, utilize hotel safes to store passports, money, and other valuables.

Prepare for an emergency by being acquainted with the emergency exits and evacuation protocols at your lodging. Make a list of nearby medical institutions and pharmacies. Stay cool in an emergency and call the right authorities or hotel personnel for help.

Respect Native Customs: Respect Kefalonia's native customs, traditions, and cultural standards. When visiting holy places, dress modestly and keep in mind local sensitivities. Learn a few simple Greek words since the locals will appreciate your efforts to converse in their language.

Stay Alert in Congested Locations: Use care in congested locations such as markets, public transit, and tourist sites. To avoid pickpocketing or theft, remain alert of your surroundings and keep a watch on your valuables.

Stay Connected: While traveling, keep your phone charged and have a dependable mode of contact. Make sure you have access to emergency numbers and vital connections in your area. It's also a good idea to provide a trusted friend or family member back home with your itinerary and contact information.

Keep Up to Date on Weather Variations: Kefalonia, like other Mediterranean resorts, may suffer weather variations. Keep up to date on weather predictions and anticipated storms or unfavorable conditions. If severe weather is forecast, listen to local authorities and take the required preparations.

Be Wary of Adventure Activities: Kefalonia has a variety of adventure activities available, including hiking, caving, and water sports. Choose trustworthy operators with skilled guides, sufficient safety equipment, and positive ratings if you want to engage in these activities. Follow all safety precautions and notify someone of your intentions.

Respect Marine Life and the Natural Environment: The natural beauty of Kefalonia is home to a broad range of marine life and habitats. Avoid harming or destroying coral reefs and marine life while participating in water activities such as snorkeling or diving. Follow ethical tourist practices such as avoiding littering and properly disposing of rubbish.

Keep Food Allergies and Dietary Restrictions in Mind: If you have food allergies or other dietary needs, be sure the restaurant staff is aware of them. Learn about typical Greek cuisines and ingredients so you can make educated decisions. Carry a card or paper in Greek that explains your dietary limitations.

Use Reliable Transit Services: When using public transit or taxis, go with licensed and reputed companies. To minimize such frauds, inquire about travel costs before beginning your trip or choose a metered taxi. If possible, pre-arrange transportation services with reputable companies or your lodging.

It's usually a good idea to keep up to date on the current health and safety situation at your destination. Before and during your journey to Kefalonia, check travel advisories, follow local rules and advice, and keep up to current on any possible health hazards or safety issues.

POPULAR SCAMS TO BE AWARE OF

When visiting Kefalonia, like with any other tourist site, it is essential to be attentive and aware of possible fraud. While Kefalonia is typically a secure destination, being aware of common scams may help you protect yourself and have a pleasant stay. As a tourist to Kefalonia, you should be alert of the following common scams:

Fake Transportation Services: When employing taxis or private transportation services, be wary. Some fraudsters act as taxi drivers, charging high prices or taking unreasonably lengthy journeys to your destination. Always check that the taxi has a functional meter or agree on a set fee ahead of time.

Fake Rental ads: If you are looking to rent a villa or apartment, be cautious of false ads on the internet. Scammers may promote appealing houses at cheap costs, request advance payments, and then vanish without giving any lodging. Before making any payments, utilize trustworthy websites, check reviews, and connect directly with the property owner or management.

Pickpockets and Street Vendors: Be wary of street sellers who may employ diversion methods to take your things in popular tourist locations or marketplaces. Keep a close check on your belongings, particularly your wallets, handbags, and cell phones. It's also a good idea to carry your bag in front of you and keep your necessities in a money belt or a safe pouch.

Fake Police Officers: Be aware of anyone who poses as police officers. They may approach you and ask for your identity or passport, claiming that there is a problem or that you have committed a crime. Before agreeing with any demands, always seek to see their identity. If you feel anything is wrong, go to the closest police station or notify local authorities.

Counterfeit Goods: Exercise caution when buying branded things at very cheap costs, especially in tourist areas or flea markets. Designer apparel, accessories, and gadgets, for example, may be marketed as genuine. Remember that if an offer seems to be too good to be true, it most often is. To confirm the authenticity of your goods, shop at reputed merchants or authorized dealers.

ATM Skimming: Be wary of ATM skimming devices, which might steal your card information. On the computer, keep an eye out for any strange attachments or loose card readers. Cover the keypad when typing your PIN to prevent others from seeing it. If you suspect tampering or strange behavior, locate another ATM or immediately notify your bank.

Fake Charity Scams: Some fraudsters may approach travelers and pose as representatives of charity groups, requesting money. While it is admirable to support real charities, it is preferable to do research and give directly to well-established and recognized organizations rather than providing money to random people.

Restaurant and Bar Scams: Some restaurants and bars may try to overcharge naive visitors, particularly if menus do not disclose costs or if pricing is opaque. Check prices before purchase and be aware of any extra costs or service fees. It's also a good idea to study reviews or get suggestions from locals to be sure you're going to a respectable place.

Scams Involving Jewelry and Gemstones: Be wary when acquiring jewelry or gemstones from street sellers or independent businesses. Some con artists may offer counterfeit or low-quality things at exorbitant costs while saying they are original or valuable. If you want to buy such products, go to a reputed jewelry shop or speak with a qualified appraiser to confirm their authenticity and worth.

Scams Using Time-Shares and Vacation Clubs: Be wary of anyone who offers free gifts or reduced vacation packages in return for attending a time-share presentation or joining a vacation club. These presentations are often high-pressure sales methods used to get you to sign hefty contracts or pay significant upfront costs. Before agreeing to anything, take the time to study and thoroughly analyze any such offers.

Scammers impersonating helpful locals or tourist information agents may give misleading or erroneous information about attractions, transportation, or hotels. To guarantee authenticity and prevent falling prey to disinformation, it is usually essential to check information from numerous sources, such as official tourist websites or certified travel firms.

Fake Tickets and Tours: Exercise caution when buying tickets for attractions, events, or tours from unlicensed sellers or internet platforms. Scammers may offer fake or illegitimate tickets, leaving you dissatisfied and out of money. Buy tickets directly from approved dealers or reliable travel companies to prevent this.

Remember that being educated, trusting your instincts, and exercising care when interacting with unknown circumstances or people are the keys to avoiding fraud. You may have a safe and pleasurable stay in Kefalonia if you are cautious and take the appropriate measures.

POPULAR ATTRACTIONS IN KEFALONIA

Here are ten popular attractions that visitors should consider exploring when in Kefalonia:

Myrtos Beach

Myrtos Beach, on Kefalonia's northwest coast, is widely regarded as one of the most beautiful beaches in Greece. Its stunning landscape, crystal-clear turquoise seas, and steep cliffs that encircle the coast enchant tourists. Myrtos Beach is described in full below:

As you reach Myrtos Beach, you'll be welcomed with a breathtaking sight: a crescent-shaped cove with white pebbles that contrast with the brilliant turquoise water. The beach is located between two huge limestone cliffs, which create a natural amphitheater and contribute to the dramatic attraction of the beach. The spectacular visual spectacle is created by the contrast between the deep blue water, the brilliant white stones, and the rich green flora on the cliffs.

As you make your way down the winding road that leads to the beach, you'll experience a surge of excitement. The sound of calm waves breaking against the coast and the refreshing aroma of the sea fills the air as you stroll onto the smooth stones. The pure waters of the beach are extraordinarily transparent, enabling you to glimpse the undersea world with extraordinary clarity.

Myrtos Beach's water is recognized for its many different colors of blue, ranging from deep sapphire to transparent turquoise. The water stays chilly and welcoming, encouraging you to take a dip and swim in its pure embrace. The beach descends gradually into the water, making it ideal for both expert swimmers and those looking to merely wade in the shallows.

Myrtos has plenty of room for sunbathers and beachgoers to relax and soak up the rays. There are sun loungers and umbrellas for hire, so you may relax comfortably while admiring the panoramic views of the Ionian Sea. Alternatively, lay your towel on the stones and soak up the warm Mediterranean sun.

While walking down the beach, you may come across little caves built into the rocks that provide shade refuge from the sun. These nooks and crannies give your stay a sense of adventure and exploration. If you're feeling more daring, rent a kayak or paddleboard and explore the shore from the sea, viewing the cliffs and coastline from a new angle.

The sun starts to set later in the day, giving a warm golden glow across the beach. This is an excellent time to see the spectacular sunset at Myrtos Beach. The sun's rays cast a wonderful shine on the countryside, converting it into a postcard-worthy image.

It's worth mentioning that Myrtos Beach is famous for its big waves, especially on windy days or when there are strong currents. It's important to be cautious and obey any safety recommendations given by lifeguards. Always be aware of the sea conditions and any warning flags that may be flying.

Melissani Cave

Melissani Cave, on the island of Kefalonia near the hamlet of Karavomylos, is a natural marvel that enchants tourists with its ethereal beauty and intriguing history. Melissani Cave is described in full below:

Melissani Cave, also known as Melissani Lake Cave, is a 1951 discovery of an underground lake cave. It is said to have developed thousands of years ago when the ceiling of a cavern collapsed, resulting in an exquisite sight that draws thousands of tourists each year.

As you approach Melissani Cave's entrance, you'll see a little gorgeous lake surrounded by rich greenery and tall trees. The entrance to the cave is a huge aperture that allows natural light to pass through and highlight the crystal-clear turquoise waters below.

Visitors explore the cave by boarding tiny rowboats that float quietly over the tranquil lake. When you get into the boat, you'll notice the hypnotic hue of the water—a stunning shade of blue that appears to shimmer when the sunlight reaches the cave's depths.

You'll enter the main chamber of Melissani Cave as the boat gently goes ahead, which opens out into a massive and awe-inspiring expanse. The roof of the cave is studded with magnificent stalactites that have grown over thousands of years, adding to the surreal ambiance.

The way sunlight penetrates Melissani Cave is the most intriguing aspect. When the sun is directly above at noon, its rays cut through a wide aperture in the cave's roof, providing an incredible sight. The water sparkles and reflects beautiful colors of the blue when the sunshine strikes it. This beautiful light show conjures feelings of enchantment and awe.

As you go further into the cave, you'll note how pure the water is, enabling you to view the underwater structures and plants. As you float over a secret world under the surface, the boat journey provides a unique viewpoint. The cave's peace and tranquility offer a soothing and even magical experience.

Melissani Cave is a natural marvel that is also rich in folklore. Local tradition has it that it was named after a nymph called Melissani who fell in love with the deity Pan. The cave is claimed to be where they used to meet in secret, providing a romantic and mysterious aspect to the already stunning environment.

Melissani Cave is an enthralling experience that mixes natural beauty, history, and a dash of legend. The ethereal lighting, dazzling blue waters, and stillness of the cave create a serene and awe-inspiring ambiance. It's a chance to immerse yourself in nature's mesmerizing marvels and make unforgettable memories.

Assos Village

Assos Village, on the northwest coast of Greece's scenic island of Kefalonia, is a quaint and enchanting place that captivates tourists' hearts with its serene beauty and ageless appeal. Assos Village is described in full below:

Assos, perched on a tiny peninsula surrounded by lush flora, emits an enchantment that takes you to another past. As you approach the hamlet, you'll be met by the sight of vivid bougainvillea flowers adorning colorful traditional homes and structures, creating a gorgeous and postcard-worthy environment.

Assos is well-known for its Venetian influences, which can be seen in the architecture and design of the buildings. The ruins of a Venetian fortification from the 16th century dominate the summit, providing panoramic views over the settlement, the Ionian Sea, and the surrounding shoreline. It's a scene that immediately catches the mind and begs to be explored.

Strolling around Assos's small streets will give you a feeling of calm and timelessness. The lack of automobiles adds to the village's tranquil atmosphere, enabling tourists to slowly explore its nooks and crannies on foot. Admire the village's particular beauty by admiring the well-preserved historic cottages with their colorful facades and wooden balconies.

Assos' port is the village's center point, presenting a gorgeous backdrop where fishing boats bob gently in the turquoise seas. You'll discover beachfront tavernas and cafés beckoning you to experience local specialties while taking in views of the sea. As you bask in the ambiance of this beachfront jewel, indulge in fresh seafood, classic Greek cuisine, and a refreshing drink.

Assos Beach, situated next to the settlement, is a little pebbly beach that is great for relaxing and unwinding. The crystal-clear waters entice you to swim, and the quiet surroundings provide a serene and private ambiance. It's the ideal spot for soaking up the rays, reading a book, or just admiring the beauty of the Ionian Sea.

A trek up to the Venetian stronghold is a must for anyone looking for a little adventure. The steep trail winds past olive orchards and provides views of the settlement below. When you get to the stronghold, you'll be greeted with spectacular panoramic views stretching as far as the eye can see. It's a photographer's dream as well as a location to connect with the region's rich heritage.

Fiskardo

Fiskardo, a lovely fishing hamlet on the northern point of the magnificent island of Kefalonia, captivates tourists with its unique combination of natural beauty, historical charm, and energetic atmosphere. Fiskardo is described in full below:

As you approach Fiskardo, you'll discover its own personality. The pastel-colored Venetian-style houses that border the shoreline make the settlement famous. These colorful buildings, some dating back to the 18th century, combine to create a charming and romantic scene that emanates old-world charm.

Fiskardo's waterfront is the hub of the community, teeming with activity. Traditional fishing boats, luxury yachts, and sailboats coexist to create a colorful and cosmopolitan ambiance. Visitors love watching the boats arrive and go while drinking a coffee or eating a meal at one of the riverside tavernas.

While strolling around Fiskardo's small alleyways, you'll come across a selection of boutique boutiques, art galleries, and trendy cafés. The community is known as an artist's paradise, drawing painters, sculptors, and crafters who are inspired by its natural beauty. Browse the stores for one-of-a-kind souvenirs, handcrafted crafts, and locally produced items.

The food scene of Fiskardo is well-known for its variety. The hamlet has a diverse selection of tavernas, restaurants, and cafés to suit all preferences. You'll discover a gastronomic pleasure for every pallet, from traditional Greek food to foreign delicacies. Enjoy freshly caught fish, local specialties, and the distinct tastes of Kefalonia.

Exploring Fiskardo's environs will lead you to quiet coves and crystal-clear seas. Explore the adjacent islands by boat, or choose a tranquil area along the shore to soak up the sun and have a refreshing dip. Fiskardo's natural beauty and environs make it a haven for nature enthusiasts and those seeking peace and quiet.

Fiskardo is also historically significant. It is one of the few communities on Kefalonia that survived the 1953 earthquake, which wrecked most of the island. As a consequence, the hamlet has kept its original architecture and beauty, giving visitors a look into the island's rich history.

The Fiskardo Maritime and Environmental Museum is a must-see for everyone interested in history and culture. The museum honors the area's maritime legacy by displaying antiques, pictures, and historical exhibits from the village's nautical past.

The lovely ambience of Fiskardo is further accentuated by its breathtaking sunsets. As the day comes to an end, locate a vantage point along the coastline or on one of the local hills to take in the beautiful hues that decorate the sky. The combination of the setting sun, the glistening sea, and the picturesque town makes an enchanting and unique experience.

Skala Beach

Skala Beach is a beautiful sandy beach that spans about 3 kilometers along Kefalonia's southeastern coast. As you approach the beach, you'll see a large stretch of soft golden sand inviting you to remove your shoes and dig your toes into its warm grains.

The beach is surrounded by beautiful natural scenery. On one side, lush green hills covered with aromatic pine trees provide a lovely background to the stunning blue waters of the Ionian Sea. The other side of the beach provides stunning views of the neighboring islands and the open sea.

The welcoming purity of Skala Beach's crystal-clear waves is well-known. The quiet and moderate waves make it an ideal location for swimming and cooling off in the water. The water progressively deepens, enabling guests of all ages to swim safely and comfortably.

Skala Beach has lots of room for sunbathers to relax and soak up the rays. Rentable sun loungers and umbrellas provide a comfy area to settle down and enjoy a day of leisure. Whether you choose to sunbathe or seek shelter beneath an umbrella, the beach provides a welcoming atmosphere for sunbathers.

Skala Beach offers a variety of beach activities for those who appreciate them. Water sports aficionados may partake in activities such as jet skiing, paddle boarding, and even parasailing. The beach is well-equipped to accommodate various activities, guaranteeing that tourists have a fun and exciting experience.

The coastline has a lively environment with a variety of beach bars, tavernas, and cafés. These restaurants provide a wide range of beverages, from cold drinks to classic Greek meals. It's the ideal time to sample delectable local food, sip a cool drink, or just take a breather from the heat while taking in the bustling atmosphere of Skala Beach.

Skala Beach takes on a distinct character when the day turns into nighttime. The seaside businesses often hold live music events and themed evenings, providing tourists with a vibrant and enjoyable ambiance. It's a chance to relax, dance to the pulse of Greek music, and enjoy Skala's dynamic nightlife.

Skala Beach is a gateway to local attractions as well as a venue for leisure and beach sports. Visitors may visit the old Roman Villa's archaeological site and marvel at its well-preserved mosaics. The neighboring Mount Ainos National Park provides trekking options as well as the opportunity to immerse yourself in the natural beauty of the island.

Mount Ainos National Park

Mount Ainos National Park, which covers roughly 28,000 acres, is a protected region that includes the beautiful Mount Ainos, Kefalonia's highest peak. The mountain, also known as "Enos," sits at an amazing 1,628 meters in height and provides stunning views of the surrounding countryside and the Ionian Sea.

The national park is a refuge for outdoor enthusiasts and wildlife lovers. It has a wide variety of vegetation and wildlife, including some rare and unique species. The slopes of Mount Ainos are covered with beautiful woods, the majority of which are made up of the island's native Abies cephalonica, or Kefalonian fir. Visitors may admire the grandeur of these towering, evergreen trees while walking through the deep forest, offering a quiet and immersive experience.

Hiking is a popular pastime at Mount Ainos National Park, and there are several routes to explore. The Park has a network of well-marked routes for people of all skill levels and inclinations. You'll be surrounded by nature's sights and sounds while you hike the paths, from birds tweeting to the soothing rustle of leaves. The beautiful landscapes along the path reward hikers with sweeping views of the island and the turquoise water, making every step worthwhile.

The trek to Mount Ainos' peak is one of the park's attractions. The trek to the summit is a difficult but rewarding experience that provides a feeling of achievement as well as amazing vistas. At the top, you'll be welcomed with a panoramic view of Kefalonia and beyond, exhibiting the island's beauty from a high vantage point.

Wildlife aficionados will be happy to learn that Mount Ainos National Park is home to a variety of animal and bird species. Wild horses, deer, foxes, and different reptiles live in the park. A variety of bird species, including the uncommon Kefalonian black pine woodpecker and golden eagles, may be seen by birdwatchers. Exploring the park with a sharp eye and a spirit of adventure may allow you to see some of these amazing species in their natural home.

Within the national park, picnic spaces and approved camping places are provided, enabling guests to enjoy a leisurely outdoor dinner or spend the night beneath the stars. Mount Ainos National Park's quiet ambience allows visitors to escape from the rush and bustle of daily life and immerse themselves in the tranquillity and serenity of nature.

Mount Ainos National Park is both a natural wonderland and a historical landmark. The Park has the remnants of a Byzantine monastery, which lends historical interest to the region. Visitors may get insight into the island's rich cultural past by exploring these historic ruins.

Argostoli

Argostoli, the capital and biggest city of Kefalonia is a dynamic and busy destination with a compelling combination of historical charm, energetic atmosphere, and breathtaking waterfront vistas.

Argostoli, on Kefalonia's southern shore, is the island's cultural, administrative, and economic hub. As you approach the city, you'll see a lovely port studded with fishing boats and yachts, providing a pleasant and welcoming image.

The Lithostroto, a pedestrianized boulevard that passes through the center of Argostoli, is one of the city's primary attractions. This busy boulevard is bordered by a mix of historic and contemporary buildings, creating a lively environment for tourists to explore. There are several boutiques, souvenir stores, cafés, and restaurants here, as well as a bustling market where you may taste local goods and socialize with the people.

Vallianos Square, the city's principal square, is a popular gathering place for both residents and visitors. This active area is surrounded by cafés and restaurants, making it a great place to unwind and have a cup of coffee or a tasty meal while taking in the lively atmosphere. The area regularly holds cultural events and live performances, contributing to the lively atmosphere of the city.

Argostoli is well-known for its historic appeal, including a number of important structures and attractions. The Korgialenios Library, located in a magnificent neoclassical edifice, is one of the city's attractions. The library has a large collection of books, manuscripts, and historical documents that provide insight into the island's rich cultural legacy.

The Drapano Bridge, commonly known as the De Bosset Bridge, is another popular site in Argostoli. This distinctive stone bridge, which originates from the nineteenth century, links the city to the opposite seashore. Walking over the bridge affords breathtaking views of the Koutavos Lagoon, where you may see a variety of birds and endangered Caretta caretta sea turtles.

Argostoli is well-known for its thriving cuisine culture. The city's eating choices vary from traditional Greek tavernas to cosmopolitan cuisine. Fresh seafood is a specialty, and you may sample a range of delectable meals prepared with locally caught fish and shellfish. Dining along the waterfront promenade with breathtaking views of the port is an unforgettable experience.

Beautiful beaches are easily accessible from the city for people seeking leisure. Makris Gialos and Platis Gialos are two famous sandy beaches just outside of Argostoli. These beaches include crystal-clear seas, beachfront amenities, and water sports activities, making them ideal for a day of sunbathing, swimming, and having fun in the sun.

Argostoli's allure stems from its unique blend of historical history, vibrant environment, and breathtaking waterfront vistas. Argostoli welcomes you to immerse yourself in its dynamic ambience and experience the real essence of Kefalonia, whether you're exploring its busy streets, eating dinner at a local taverna, or walking along the scenic port.

Assos Castle

Assos Castle, also known as St. George's Castle, is situated in the picturesque town of Assos on Kefalonia's northwest coast. The castle, which dates back to the 16th century, is a tribute to the island's turbulent past as well as the strategic significance of its position.

Assos Castle's strong appearance and lovely environment will strike you as you approach it. The castle is perched on a hill above Assos town, providing panoramic views of the Ionian Sea, the beautiful surrounding landscape, and the picturesque hamlet below.

Visitors may approach the castle by taking a leisurely walk along a meandering road that winds between olive orchards and wildflowers. The climb allows you to take in the natural splendor of the region while also enjoying the tranquil atmosphere. You may also drive up to the castle, where parking is provided nearby.

When you arrive at the castle, you will be surprised by its well-preserved defenses, which include large stone walls and strong towers. As you walk around the castle grounds, you will see relics of historic buildings and structures that originally performed different tasks inside the castle complex. Exploring the castle transports you back in time, allowing you to picture the lives of individuals who lived and guarded it centuries ago.

The stunning view from Assos Castle's lofty elevation is one of its features. The blue waters of the Ionian Sea, the craggy shoreline, and the picturesque settlement of Assos can all be seen from the castle walls. The sweeping panoramas are most captivating at sunset when the sky is painted with orange and pink colors, creating a magnificent light over the area.

You'll come across the ruins of a Venetian church, a Turkish mosque, and an ancient jail as you tour the castle. These constructions provide a look into the castle's history as well as the numerous cultural influences that have impacted the island throughout time.

Aside from its historical importance, Assos Castle has a peaceful and calm ambiance. The tranquility of the surroundings, along with the breathtaking vistas, make it a great location for introspection and thought. Many tourists opt to carry a picnic and have a leisurely dinner while admiring the scenery.

Visiting Assos Castle allows you to see the picturesque hamlet of Assos as well. The community is well-known for its medieval architecture, tiny lanes, and brightly colored buildings. Wander the village's meandering streets, browse at local stores, and dine at one of the tavernas, where you may experience traditional Greek meals and fresh fish.

Assos Castle is a must-see for history buffs, nature lovers, and those looking for a peaceful vacation on the island of Kefalonia. Its historical importance, breathtaking vistas, and tranquil ambience combine to produce an unforgettable experience for anybody who comes.

Lighthouse of Saint Theodoroi

The Lighthouse of Saint Theodoroi, located near the hamlet of Argostoli, rises boldly on a steep cliff at the entrance to the natural harbor. The British built the lighthouse in 1828, and it has functioned as a guiding beacon for sailors traveling the dangerous waters of the Ionian Sea for generations.

The lighthouse is named for Saint Theodoroi, the patron saint of sailors, and serves as a sign of safety and protection for people at sea. Its placement on Kefalonia's northernmost point makes it a notable landmark and an iconic emblem of the island.

As tourists approach the lighthouse, they are met with a spectacular building that towers over the surrounding countryside. The lighthouse itself is a white-painted stone cylindrical tower with a crimson lantern chamber on top. The tower is very tall, providing a commanding perspective of the surrounding region.

Visitors may reach the Lighthouse of Saint Theodoroi by following a winding route that goes to the cliff's edge. The panoramic views gradually expand as you rise, highlighting the turquoise seas of the Ionian Sea, the gorgeous shoreline, and the towering cliffs that flank the beach. The trek to the lighthouse is an adventure in and of itself, offering vistas of Kefalonia's natural splendor.

Visitors to the lighthouse are rewarded with breathtaking views in every direction. The expanse of the sea, the adjacent island of Ithaca, and the beautiful flora that covers the island may all be seen from the lofty vantage. The vistas are especially beautiful around sunset, when the golden colors of the sky contrast with the deep blue water, producing a hypnotic display of colors.

Aside from its lovely site and spectacular views, the Saint Theodoroi Lighthouse has historical value. It has watched the passage of innumerable ships, played an important part in nautical navigation, and served as a symbol of hope for sailors throughout the years. Visitors may enjoy the lighthouse's architectural splendor and learn about its rich history by exploring it.

The region around the lighthouse is extremely popular among environmental enthusiasts and photographers. The dramatic and awe-inspiring sight is created by the steep cliffs and smashing waves against the rocks. Visitors may enjoy leisurely walks along the cliffside walkways, soaking in the beauty of the surroundings and reveling in the tranquility of the setting.

The Saint Theodoroi Lighthouse is not only a historical monument but also a haven of peace and introspection. The breathtaking sights and tranquil environment make it a great location for introspection, meditation, or just admiring nature's splendor.

Visiting the Saint Theodoroi Lighthouse enables you to connect with the island's nautical heritage, experience panoramic perspectives, and immerse yourself in Kefalonia's enchanting nature.

Saint Gerasimos Monastery

The Saint Gerasimos Monastery, nestled in the peaceful countryside, emanates peace and spiritual devotion. The monastery is placed in a verdant valley surrounded by olive groves, cypress trees, and vineyards, providing a scenic environment that contributes to the monastery's tranquil aura.

The monastery is named after Saint Gerasimos, a revered 16th-century saint. Saint Gerasimos is noted for his miracles and dedication to community service. His relics, including his mummified corpse, are kept at the monastery, which is a popular pilgrimage destination for Orthodox Christians.

Visitors are met by the monastery's spectacular entry gate, which is covered with elaborate carvings and religious motifs. The complex is made up of various structures, including the main church, chapels, monks' cells, a museum, and a bakery.

The main church, dedicated to Saint Gerasimos, is a lovely edifice with Byzantine characteristics. Inside, visitors may observe beautiful paintings and icons depicting scenes from the saint's and other holy luminaries' lives. The church's environment is reverent and serene, enabling guests to ponder and find consolation in their spiritual journey.

A little chapel known as the "Old Church" is located next to the church. Pilgrims and tourists may worship and reflect in this chapel, which holds the saint's remains. The remains of Saint Gerasimos are said to have healing abilities, and many people come to seek consolation, pray, and get blessings.

The monastery also has a museum with a collection of holy relics such as old manuscripts, icons, vestments, and things relating to Saint Gerasimos' life and miracles. The museum provides visitors with insights into the monastery's history and importance, as well as a fuller knowledge of the Orthodox Christian religion.

A bakery next to the museum produces traditional bread and pastries made by the monks. The bakery is famous for its delectable sweets, notably the "makarounes," a sweet pasta-like confection created and sold by the monks as a source of nutrition and to help fund the monastery's activities.

Visiting the Saint Gerasimos Monastery provides both a spiritual experience and a chance to observe the natural beauty of the surrounding region. The monastery sits in the Omala Valley, which is famous for its beautiful soil and lush foliage. Visitors may interact with nature and enjoy the tranquility of the surroundings by walking around the monastery grounds and adjoining olive fields.

The Saint Gerasimos Monastery has a unique place in the hearts of the locals, who commemorate the saint's feast day on August 16th with great devotion and delight. The feast day draws a huge number of pilgrims and tourists who come to participate in religious services, see traditional traditions, and enjoy the festive atmosphere.

A visit to the Saint Gerasimos Monastery allows visitors to immerse themselves in the island's religious tradition, connect with spirituality, and observe the natural beauty of the island.

OFF-THE-BEATEN-PATH DESTINATIONS

Katelios Village: Located on Kefalonia's southern coast, Katelios is a picturesque fishing community famed for its relaxed attitude and magnificent beaches. It provides an insight into typical Greek island life.

Kato Kateleios Beach: A secluded sanctuary with crystal-clear seas and quiet surroundings, Kato Kateleios Beach is a hidden treasure near Katelios. It's a great place to unwind and be alone.

Lourdas Beach is a magnificent expanse of golden sand surrounded by spectacular cliffs on the southern coast. It's a calm beach with fewer people, ideal for sunbathing and relaxing in peace.

Agia Paraskevi Beach is a hidden treasure on the Paliki Peninsula, with blue waves and a quiet ambience. The beach has spectacular vistas and is frequently less crowded than the island's other famous beaches.

Spartia Beach: Spartia Beach is a lovely cove on the southern coast with tranquil waves and a quiet environment. It's an ideal location for swimming and sunbathing in a tranquil atmosphere.

Alaties Beach: Alaties Beach is a tiny, quiet cove near the hamlet of Agia Efimia with crystal-clear seas and colorful rocks. It's a hidden treasure that provides a peaceful respite.

Vouti Beach: A tiny and quiet bay encircled by rocks; Vouti Beach is a hidden treasure on the Paliki Peninsula. With its pristine seas filled with marine life, it's a perfect area for relaxing and snorkeling.

Kardakata Cave: Kardakata Cave is a hidden natural marvel near the hamlet of Karavados. It has magnificent rock formations and stalactites, and exploring its depths is a once-in-a-lifetime experience.

Mount Enos: As Kefalonia's tallest peak, Mount Enos provides stunning views and trekking options.

The mountain is home to a rare kind of fir trees and is a naturalist's and adventurer's dream.

Agios Dimitrios Monastery: Nestled among olive trees near the town of Pessada, the Agios Dimitrios Monastery is a hidden gem. The quiet atmosphere and stunning architecture make it a spiritual and pleasant place to visit.

Skala Castle Remains: The castle remains, located near the settlement of Skala, provide a look into the island's medieval past. The position provides panoramic views of the surrounding region, making it an ideal location for photographers.

Kaminia Beach is a peaceful and isolated place on the southern coast famed for its golden sand and shallow seas. It's a great option for families with children and those looking for peace and quiet.

Fteri Beach: Tucked away on the Paliki Peninsula, Fteri Beach is a hidden treasure that can only be reached by boat or a difficult climb. Its pure beauty, blue seas, and distinctive rock formations make it a popular destination for daring vacationers.

Mavratzis Beach: Mavratzis Beach is a quiet pebble beach surrounded by rocks on the northeastern shore. Away from the crowded tourist districts, it's a perfect setting for solitude and leisure.

Koutavos Lagoon: The Koutavos Lagoon is a quiet natural reserve near Argostoli with abundant birds and lovely walking pathways. It's a secret haven in the center of the city, ideal for nature lovers.

OUTDOOR ACTIVITIES AND EXPERIENCES

Here are some of Kefalonia's best outdoor activities and experiences:

Hiking & Trekking: Kefalonia has a plethora of magnificent trails and routes that wind across its mountains, valleys, and shoreline. Mount Ainos National Park is a popular hiking location, with paths of varied difficulty levels. Explore the deep woods of the park, discover rare flora and wildlife, and take in the beautiful vistas from the mountain's peak.

Beach Hopping: Kefalonia has several beautiful beaches due to its scenic coastline. From well-known beaches like Myrtos and Skala to lesser-known treasures like Petanoi and Platia Ammos, you can spend your days exploring the different coastal landscapes, swimming in crystal-clear seas, and soaking up the Mediterranean sun.

Scuba Diving and Snorkeling: Go scuba diving or snorkeling to explore Kefalonia's beautiful underwater environment. The clean waters of the island provide good visibility, and you may explore unique dive spots filled with marine life, vivid coral reefs, and underwater caverns. Several diving facilities and tour companies in Kefalonia provide guided dives and snorkeling tours for divers of various levels of expertise.

Sea Kayaking: Set out on a sea kayaking excursion along Kefalonia's scenic coastline. Glide through turquoise waves, discover secret coves and sea caves, and gaze in awe at the stunning cliffs and rock formations. There are guided trips offered, which include equipment, training, and the opportunity to visit isolated areas only accessible by kayak.

Boat Tours and Sailing: Take a boat tour or a sailing adventure to see Kefalonia from the water. Cruise around the coast, stopping at distant beaches and secret coves to appreciate the magnificent cliffs and harsh landscapes of the island. You may also go sailing and visit the neighboring islands of Ithaca, Meganisi, and Zakynthos.

Horseback Riding: Discover secret routes, olive orchards, and lovely towns while riding across the landscape of the island. Several equestrian facilities in Kefalonia provide guided horseback riding trips for riders of various levels of expertise, enabling you to appreciate the island's natural beauty from a new viewpoint.

Caving: Explore the island's caverns to learn about its hidden treasures. Melissani Cave and Drogarati Cave are two renowned tourist locations. Admire the spectacular stalactite and stalagmite formations, explore huge caves, and learn about the island's geological history.

Bird Watching: Kefalonia is home to a variety of bird species, making it a bird watcher's delight. The Koutavos Lagoon, Livadi Marsh, and Mount Ainos are ideal places to see birds like as herons, flamingos, and buzzards. Bring your binoculars and explore these natural settings to see the island's avifauna.

Paragliding: Enjoy stunning aerial views of Kefalonia's scenery while experiencing the excitement of paragliding. Take off from authorized launch points and fly over the island, admiring its beautiful coastline, mountains, and colorful flora from a new viewpoint. Tandem flights are offered for people who have never flown a paraglider before.

Jeep Safaris: Take a thrilling jeep safari experience through Kefalonia's rocky landscape and secret places. Explore off-road trails, go through woods and mountains, and visit distant settlements and scenic views. Jeep safari trips provide a unique combination of excitement, discovery, and cultural immersion.

Rock Climbing: The rocky terrain of Kefalonia provides chances for rock climbing and bouldering. The island's cliffs and crags offer a tough but rewarding experience for climbers of all skill levels. Climbing trips and classes for both beginners and expert climbers are provided.

Olive Oil Tasting and Harvesting: Participate in olive oil tasting and harvesting events to immerse yourself in Kefalonia's rich agricultural tradition. Visit historic olive trees, learn about the olive oil manufacturing process, and experience the flavors of premium extra virgin olive oil.

Wine Tours: Take a wine tour through Kefalonia's vineyards and wineries to learn about the island's winemaking traditions and sample a selection of local wines. Visit family-run estates, wander through vineyards, and partake in wine-tasting sessions while taking in the scenery.

Yoga & Wellness Retreats: The tranquil settings of Kefalonia are suitable for wellness retreats and yoga sessions. Participate in a retreat or yoga lessons given in scenic locales such as beaches or overlooking the sea. Relax, rejuvenate, and reconnect with nature in a peaceful setting.

Sunset Chasing: Kefalonia boasts some of the best sunsets in the world, and there are several vantage points from which to capture these spectacular moments. Witnessing the beautiful hues of the setting sun is a wonderful experience, whether from a cliffside perspective, a beachside taverna, or a boat in the water.

NEARBY DAY TRIPS FROM KEFALONIA

Kefalonia's location in the Ionian Sea makes it an ideal starting point for visiting the neighboring islands and other mainland sites. If you want to go on a day excursion outside of Kefalonia, there are various interesting places to visit. Here are some suggestions for day excursions from Kefalonia:

Ithaca: The nearby island of Ithaca is a great day trip option and is just a short boat ride away. Ithaca, the fabled home of Odysseus, provides a tranquil and untouched atmosphere. Visit Vathy's scenic port, the Cave of the Nymphs, and the island's lovely beaches and hiking paths.

Zakynthos (Zante): Zakynthos, another popular Ionian Island, is known for its breathtaking sceneries, notably the famed Navagio Beach with its shipwreck. Take a boat ride to visit the famed beach, swim in the crystal-clear waters of the Blue Caves, and explore Zakynthos Town, the island's picturesque capital.

Lefkada: A short ferry ride or spectacular drive across the floating bridge will take you to Lefkada, which has beautiful beaches, attractive towns, and dramatic terrain. Relax on the world-famous Porto Katsiki Beach, discover the lovely village of Nidri, and hike the spectacular Cape Lefkatas cliffs.

Kalamata: For a lengthier day excursion, go to the mainland and see the bustling city of Kalamata. Kalamata, in the Peloponnese area, is well-known for its olives and olive oil. Explore the old district, pay a visit to the Archaeological Museum, and take a walk along the gorgeous coastline promenade.

Island Hopping in Fiscardo, Ithaca, and Lefkada: For a more immersive experience, combine trips to Fiscardo in Kefalonia, Vathy in Ithaca, and Nydri in Lefkada on an island-hopping journey. These three lovely ports provide a look into each island's own personality, as well as stunning landscapes and idyllic beaches.

Mainland Greece: If you have more time to travel, you may go deeper into mainland Greece. Consider visiting Ancient Olympia, the origin of the Olympic Games, or Delphi, famous for its archaeological remains and the Oracle of Delphi.

Acheron River and Necromanteion: Located on the mainland in the Epirus area, the Acheron River and Necromanteion provide a magical and wonderful day excursion. Visit the ancient Necromanteion, an archaeological site linked with the Underworld and ancient ceremonies, and explore the mythological river and its gorgeous natural environs.

Another mainland journey brings you to the enthralling **Blue Eye Spring** (Syvota Springs) and the gorgeous seaside village of Syvota. Enjoy the beautiful splendor of Syvota's coastline, with its quaint port and traditional tavernas, as well as the brilliant blue waters of the natural spring.

Corfu: Located farther north in the Ionian Sea, Corfu is an enticing day excursion from Kefalonia. Corfu, known for its Venetian architecture, attractive Old Town, and magnificent beaches, combines history, culture, and natural beauty. Explore the Old Town's tiny alleyways, pay a visit to the Achilleion Palace, and unwind on one of the island's gorgeous beaches.

Parga: Located on the mainland's northwest coast, the town of Parga is a beautiful day trip location. Parga radiates beauty and individuality with its colorful buildings, small alleyways, and hilltop fortification. Stroll along the waterfront promenade, relax on the town's lovely beaches, and take in the panoramic views from the Venetian Castle.

Blue Caves of Zante (Zakynthos): If you want to see more of Zakynthos than Navagio Beach, a boat journey to the Blue Caves is an excellent alternative. The bright blue tones formed by sunlight bouncing off the water distinguish these stunning sea caves. Swim in the crystal-clear waters and observe the unusual rock formations on a guided boat excursion.

Kastos and Kalamos: These two little islands off the east coast of Kefalonia are ideal for a relaxing day excursion. Explore Kastos' quaint town, scenic harbor, and peaceful beaches. Then, go to Kalamos, which is famous for its unspoiled natural beauty and hiking routes. Enjoy the peace and quiet of these islands, away from the bustle of major tourist spots.

Meganisi: Just a short boat trip from Nydri in Lefkada, Meganisi provides a tranquil respite. Discover secret coves, swim on isolated beaches, and relax on this pristine island's laid-back vibe. You may explore Meganisi's coastline and nearby islands by renting a boat or joining a boat excursion.

Papanikolis Cave: A magnificent sea cave named after a Greek submarine; Papanikolis Cave is located near the port of Spartochori on Meganisi. The cave, which is only accessible by boat, is noted for its breathtaking rock formations and the interaction of light and water. Take a boat excursion to explore the depths of the cave and admire its natural beauty.

Keri Caves: Located on Zakynthos' southwest shore, the Keri Caves are a hidden treasure worth investigating. Join a boat excursion to explore these magnificent sea caverns, which are distinguished by their spectacular rock formations, pure turquoise seas, and secret tunnels. The boat cruises often include swimming and snorkeling stops in the neighboring Turtle Island Bay.

These day tours from Kefalonia allow you to see more of the Ionian Islands and surrounding mainland sites. From medieval cities to spectacular natural beauties, each site has its own distinct appeal and attraction, improving your entire Kefalonia experience.

A PERFECT SEVEN-DAY ITINERARY FOR A VISIT TO KEFALONIA

A 7-day itinerary for a visit to Kefalonia allows you to explore the island's diverse landscapes, picturesque villages, stunning beaches, and cultural heritage. Here's a detailed day-by-day itinerary to help you make the most of your time on this beautiful Greek island:

Day 1: Arrival in Argostoli and City Exploration

Arrive in Kefalonia and settle into your accommodation in the island's capital, Argostoli.

Take a leisurely stroll along the waterfront promenade, Lithostroto Street, and Vallianos Square.

Visit the Korgialenio Historic and Folklore Museum to learn about Kefalonia's history and culture.

Enjoy a meal at a local taverna, savoring traditional Greek cuisine.

Day 2: Myrtos Beach and Assos Village

Begin your day with a visit to Myrtos Beach, one of the most iconic beaches in Greece. Relax on the white pebble shoreline and admire the turquoise waters.

Afterward, drive to the charming village of Assos. Explore its narrow streets, visit the Venetian castle ruins, and enjoy panoramic views of the Ionian Sea.

Have dinner at a seaside taverna in Assos, sampling fresh seafood dishes.

Day 3: Melissani Cave and Fiskardo

Start your day with a visit to Melissani Cave. Take a boat ride on the underground lake, marvel at the stunning rock formations, and enjoy the magical play of sunlight inside the cave.

Head north to Fiskardo, a picturesque fishing village known for its colorful houses and charming harbor.

Explore the village, browse boutique shops, and dine at one of the waterfront restaurants.

Day 4: Boat Trip to Ithaca

Embark on a day trip to the neighboring island of Ithaca. Take a ferry from Sami to Vathy, the capital of Ithaca.

Explore Vathy's charming streets, visit the Archaeological Museum, and enjoy a leisurely lunch at a local taverna.

Discover the legendary Cave of the Nymphs and explore the picturesque village of Kioni.

Return to Kefalonia in the evening and enjoy a relaxing dinner in Argostoli.

Day 5: Beach-Hopping and Sea Kayaking

Spend the day exploring Kefalonia's stunning beaches. Start with Skala Beach, known for its long sandy shoreline and crystal-clear waters.

Continue to Petanoi Beach, a secluded gem nestled between dramatic cliffs.

In the afternoon, embark on a sea kayaking adventure. Paddle along the coast, explore hidden coves, and discover the island's rugged beauty from a unique perspective.

Enjoy a sunset dinner at a beachfront taverna.

Day 6: Mount Ainos and Robola Wine Tasting

Take a scenic drive to Mount Ainos National Park.

Hike through the park's trails, enjoying the lush greenery and panoramic views from the summit.

Afterward, visit a local winery and indulge in a wine-tasting session of Robola, a unique grape variety grown in Kefalonia.

Return to Argostoli and spend the evening exploring the city's nightlife, visiting lively bars and cafes.

Day 7: Lighthouse of Saint Theodoroi and Lassi Beach

Start your day with a visit to the Lighthouse of Saint Theodoroi near Argostoli. Enjoy panoramic views of the coastline and the turquoise waters of the Ionian Sea.

Head to Lassi Beach, a popular stretch of coastline known for its golden sand and shallow waters. Take it easy at the beach, go for a dip in the ocean, and get some sun.

In the evening, enjoy a farewell dinner at a waterfront restaurant, savoring delicious Greek cuisine and reflecting on your memorable time in Kefalonia.

This 7-day itinerary provides a balanced mix of relaxation, exploration, natural beauty, and cultural experiences, allowing you to discover the best of Kefalonia. However, feel free to adjust the itinerary based on your preferences and add additional activities or destinations to tailor it to your interests.

CULTURAL FESTIVALS AND HOLIDAYS

The island comes alive throughout the year with festivities, rituals, and events that highlight Kefalonia's rich cultural past. Here are some of the prominent festivals and holidays to be found in Kefalonia:

Feast of Agios Gerasimos (August 16th): This is one of the most major religious events on the island, honoring Saint Gerasimos, Kefalonia's patron saint. Pilgrims from all over Greece come to pay their respects and seek blessings at the monastery of Agios Gerasimos, near the town of Valsamata. Religious processions, liturgies, and a festive atmosphere with traditional music, dancing, and local specialties are all part of the celebration.

Carnival (February/March): The carnival season in Kefalonia is distinguished by vibrant parades, colorful costumes, and joyful festivities. Music, dancing, and theatrical performances fill the streets of Argostoli and other large towns. The "Robola

Wine Festival" in February is the carnival's high point, with residents and tourists alike gathering to enjoy wine tastings, traditional dances, and live music.

Wine Festivals: Kefalonia is well-known for its fine wines, and a number of wine festivals are conducted throughout the year to commemorate the island's winemaking legacy. The most notable is the "Robola Wine Festival" in Fragata in early August. Visitors may sample the famed Robola wine, dance, and participate in cultural activities.

Kefalonia holds a number of **music events** that feature both local and international talent. During the summer months, the "Kefalonia Music Festival" is a well-known event that takes place in different locations around the island. It hosts classical music, opera, and chamber music events, drawing music lovers from all over the globe.

Easter is an important religious event in Greece, and Kefalonia celebrates it with tremendous dedication and tradition. Church services, processions, and symbolic ceremonies occupy the Holy Week leading up to Easter Sunday. The epitaph processions in Argostoli and neighboring towns are especially striking on Good Friday, with residents carrying lighted candles and chanting hymns.

Panigiri Festivals: Panigiri festivals are traditional festivities celebrated throughout the year in local villages, frequently related to the village's patron saint. Live music, dancing, traditional costumes, and an abundance of local cuisine and wine are all part of these celebrations. They provide an excellent chance to learn about the original local culture and interact with the friendly islanders.

Independence Day (March 25th): On March 25th, Kefalonia, like the rest of Greece, celebrates its independence. The day marks the beginning of the Greek War of Independence in 1821. Argostoli hosts the primary celebrations, which include a military parade, schoolchildren's plays, and patriotic speeches.

Cultural Events in Agia Efimia: Throughout the summer, the lovely hamlet of Agia Efimia holds a variety of cultural events and festivals. Music concerts, theater performances, art displays, and traditional dances are among the festivities. Visitors may immerse themselves in the village's lovely ambience while immersing themselves in the local arts and culture scene.

Ascension of the Virgin Mary (August 15th): This holy festival commemorates the Ascension of the Virgin Mary and is extensively celebrated in Kefalonia. Church services, processions, and feasts are held on this day. The Panagia Themata Monastery, near Markopoulo hamlet, hosts the most important festival. Pilgrims go to the monastery to pay their respects to the Virgin Mary and take part in religious rites.

While not a traditional festival or holiday, **the nesting season of the endangered loggerhead sea turtles (Caretta caretta)** is a unique and very important occurrence in Kefalonia. These lovely animals' nest on the beaches of the island, notably on the Lixouri Peninsula and the southern shore. Visitors may see the nesting process and, later in the season, the hatching of the young turtles. To promote awareness about sea turtle protection, many conservation groups provide guided tours and educational activities.

Kefalonia and Ithaca International Music Festival: The International Music Festival, held yearly in July and August, brings together famous musicians and artists from across the globe. Classical, jazz, and traditional Greek music are among the genres represented in the event. Concerts are held in ancient sites, cathedrals, and open-air amphitheaters, providing music fans with a one-of-a-kind cultural experience.

Panagia Agrilion Feast (September 8th): This religious celebration honors Panagia Agrilion, the Virgin Mary of the Wild. The ceremony takes place at Agrilias, a hamlet in Kefalonia's Paliki district. Visitors may see the procession of the Panagia Agrilion image, which is accompanied by religious chanting and traditional music. Food vendors selling local specialties live music performances, and dancing round off the celebrations.

Wine Harvest Festivals: The vineyards of Kefalonia come alive during the wine harvest season, which takes place in September and October. Several vineyards have harvest festivals where visitors may trample grapes, sample freshly squeezed grape juice, and learn about the winemaking process. These events provide a one-of-a-kind chance to learn about the island's viticulture traditions and sample the tastes of freshly picked grapes.

Feasts of Local Saints: Throughout the island, there are various little churches dedicated to local saints. These churches organize feasts to commemorate their individual saints throughout the year. These small-scale festivals provide a look at the island's agricultural culture and traditions. Visitors may participate in religious processions with the locals, sample local cuisine and wine, and feel the warmth and welcome of the Kefalonian community.

Olive Harvest: The olive harvest season, which normally lasts from late fall to early January, is critical for the island's agricultural population. Locals gather in the olive orchards to harvest the olives and manufacture the island's famed extra virgin olive oil. Visitors may select their own olives, see historic olive presses, and learn about the olive oil manufacturing process. It's a terrific chance to get hands-on with agriculture and learn about the importance of olive production in Kefalonia.

BEST BEACHES IN KEFALONIA

Kefalonia is famous for its gorgeous beaches, which have crystal-clear blue seas, silky golden sands, and spectacular natural settings. Here are some of Kefalonia's top beaches, each with its own distinct charm and beauty:

Myrtos Beach: With its spectacular cliffs, white pebbles, and deep blue seas, Myrtos Beach is without a doubt one of Greece's most famous beaches. Nestled amid towering mountains, it provides a captivating setting for sunbathing, swimming, and admiring the view.

Petani Beach: Petani Beach, located on the Paliki Peninsula, enchants tourists with its exquisite white beaches and vivid blue waves. This picturesque beach, surrounded by lush green hills, offers a calm and isolated setting ideal for relaxing and snorkeling.

Antisamos Beach: Known for its appearance in the film "Captain Corelli's Mandolin," Antisamos Beach is stunning in its natural beauty. The beach is surrounded by high green hills and provides a mix of pebbles and sand, and the brilliant blue seas are great for swimming and water sports.

Xi Beach: Xi Beach is notable for its distinctive reddish-brown sand and shallow, mild seas. This kid-friendly beach is famous for its natural clay cliffs, where tourists may enjoy natural mud treatments. The shallow and tranquil water is ideal for youngsters to play and swim in.

Skala Beach is a long expanse of golden sand and pebbles bordered by seaside tavernas and cafés. It is a popular destination for sunbathing, swimming, and water sports due to its pristine waters and Blue Flag classification. The beach is well-equipped and provides breathtaking views of the adjacent islands.

Makris Gialos Beach: Makris Gialos Beach is a sandy beach with crystal-clear seas located near the tourist town of Lassi. Its dynamic and active environment, as well as many beach bars and water sports facilities, make it a popular destination for both residents and visitors looking for a fun-filled day at the beach.

Lourdas Beach: Lourdas Beach spans along a lovely bay with lush cliffs and undulating hills as a background. The long sandy beach is surrounded by rich greenery, providing a tranquil and pleasant atmosphere. Swimming and sunbathing are perfect due to the calm waters and easy slope.

Ammes Beach is a tiny, family-friendly beach situated near the airport. It is perfect for young children because to its golden sand and shallow seas. The beach has sun loungers, umbrellas, and a taverna on the beach where tourists may enjoy a cool drink or a nice meal.

Avithos Beach: Avithos Beach is a hidden treasure on Kefalonia's southern shore. It offers a calm and natural vacation with its beautiful golden beaches, crystal-clear seas, and lush flora. The beach is well-known for its beautiful sunsets, making it a great location for evening strolls.

Platis Gialos Beach: Tucked away in a little cove, Platis Gialos Beach is a peaceful and lovely beach. It provides a feeling of privacy and tranquility since it is surrounded by tall cliffs and rich flora. The clean waters and pebbly beach are ideal for snorkeling and observing marine life.

KEFALONIA FOR FAMILIES

Kefalonia is an excellent family vacation destination, combining natural beauty, family-friendly activities, and a warm and inviting attitude. The island is great for a family holiday since it offers a secure and enjoyable environment for children to explore, play, and learn. Here is a more in-depth look at what Kefalonia has to offer families:

Beaches: Kefalonia is well-known for its beautiful beaches with clean seas and smooth sands, many of which are excellent for families with children. Skala, Lourdas, and Ammes beaches have shallow and calm seas, making them ideal for children to swim and play. For your convenience, these beaches provide facilities such as sunbeds, umbrellas, and beachside tavernas.

Outdoor Experiences: Kefalonia's natural terrain provides several chances for family outdoor experiences. Hiking routes, such as the one to Mount Ainos, allow visitors to discover the picturesque splendor of the island. Boat cruises are available for families to explore secret coves, marine caves, and snorkeling areas. The rough coastline of the island also provides opportunities for water kayaking and paddleboarding.

Water Sports: Families looking for adventure and water-based sports in Kefalonia can discover a variety of possibilities. Jet skiing, banana boat rides, and parasailing are among the activities available at water sports establishments in popular beach regions such as Skala and Lassi. These activities are likely to leave a lasting impression on both youngsters and adults.

Family-Friendly Accommodation: Kefalonia has a variety of family-friendly accommodations. There are options to suit all budgets and interests, ranging from family-friendly hotels and resorts to self-catering villas and apartments. Many hotels provide amenities such as swimming pools, children's play spaces, and scheduled entertainment to ensure that families have a pleasant and pleasurable visit.

Animal Encounters: Kefalonia offers youngsters the opportunity to interact with nature and animals. Visitors may engage in turtle conservation initiatives or join guided excursions to view the nesting or hatching of endangered loggerhead sea turtles on the island. The neighboring Ainos National Park is an excellent area for children to learn about the island's flora and animals.

Attractions for Families: Kefalonia has various attractions designed exclusively for families. Children may learn about and interact with rescued creatures including owls, reptiles, and more at the Kefalonia Wildlife Sense Park in Lakithra. The Aquatic Diving Center in Lassi allows kids to practice scuba diving in a regulated and safe atmosphere.

Kefalonia's rich cultural legacy may be explored via a variety of family-friendly activities. Families may take in the authentic Greek island vibe by exploring the lovely towns of Assos and Fiskardo. Taking children to local markets and serving them traditional

Greek food is a great way to expose them to different sensations and culinary experiences.

Kefalonia is noted for its friendly and inviting attitude, with residents who really love interacting with guests. The island is regarded as secure for travelers, and families may feel at ease visiting its cities, villages, and natural wonders.

Kefalonia is easily accessible by air and sea, with direct flights and ferry connections from Athens and other major Greek towns. The size of the island allows families to visit various regions without having to drive vast distances.

Kefalonia's eateries and tavernas often welcome families with open arms. Many restaurants include kid-friendly menus, high seats, and outside dining spaces where kids may play while their parents dine. With its fresh ingredients and tasty meals, Greek food often appeals to children's palates.

Kefalonia has a multitude of family-friendly experiences, combining breathtaking natural beauty, exciting activities, and a kind environment. The island assures that families have a memorable and fun vacation together with its broad choice of activities and hotels.

Practical Tips and Recommendations for Traveling with Kids

Traveling to Kefalonia with children may be a beautiful and unforgettable experience. Here are some practical ideas and advice to make your journey as seamless and pleasurable as possible:

Plan Ahead of Time: Before visiting Kefalonia, look into family-friendly activities, attractions, and lodgings. Make a flexible plan that incorporates beach days, outdoor excursions, and cultural events that are appropriate for children.

Choose Family-Friendly Accommodation: Look for family-friendly accommodation. Swimming pools, children's play spaces, and planned entertainment are common features of family-friendly hotels and resorts. Families may find self-catering villas or apartments with cooking amenities to be a handy alternative.

Pack Essentials: Don't forget to bring sunscreen, caps, bug repellent, swim diapers, and appropriate walking shoes for your children. Bring any essential prescriptions as well as a basic first aid kit.

Stay Hydrated: Because Kefalonia may get hot in the summer, it's critical to keep your family hydrated. Carry water bottles and urge your children to drink often, particularly while spending time outside.

Protect your children from the sun's damaging rays by using sunscreen on a regular basis, even on overcast days. To protect their skin, they should wear hats, sunglasses, and UV-protective clothes. During the warmest hours of the day, seek shade.

Keep a Watch on Your Children at the Beach: When visiting the beaches of Kefalonia, keep a watch on your children at all times. Make sure kids remain in authorized swimming areas and provide them with floating gear if necessary. Teach kids about water safety and the necessity of following lifeguard directions.

Embrace Local Cuisine: Kefalonia has a diverse culinary scene, and eating local foods may be a fun and informative activity for kids. Introduce them to traditional Greek dishes such as moussaka, souvlaki, Greek salads, and fresh fish. Look for eateries with kid-friendly menus or ask locals for ideas.

Allow Your Children to Participate in the Planning: Allow your children to have a voice in the activities and attractions you visit. Allow them to select a few activities that interest them, such as visiting a certain beach, touring a community, or attempting a new water activity. Involving kids in the preparation phase builds enthusiasm and keeps them interested during the vacation.

Maintain a Flexible Schedule: While having a plan is important, be flexible and adjust to your children's demands and energy levels. Allow for rest, relaxation, and unexpected discoveries. Remember that traveling with children may need adjusting your pace and expectations.

Participate in Educational Activities: Kefalonia provides a variety of educational options. Children may learn about the island's history, culture, and ecology by visiting museums, historical sites, and natural parks. Participate in family-friendly guided tours or workshops to make learning more dynamic and interesting.

Take Advantage of Local Services: Kefalonia offers plenty of supermarkets, pharmacies, and medical facilities. If you want supplies or medical attention, don't be afraid to contact locals or your lodging staff for advice and help.

Accept the Island's Pace: Kefalonia offers a laid-back and comfortable vibe. Accept the slower pace of the island and make time to be with your family. Allow your kids to play in the sand, discover rock pools, and engage with local kids to make lifelong experiences.

By following these suggestions, you may assure a memorable and fun holiday with your children in Kefalonia. The natural beauty of the island, as well as the family-friendly activities and welcoming welcome, make it a perfect place for a fun-filled family holiday.

KEFALONIA FOR COUPLES

Kefalonia is an ideal romantic weekend resort for couples. The island's breathtaking natural beauty, beautiful communities, and personal encounters make it ideal for a memorable couple's holiday. Here are some fun things to do in Kefalonia with your partner:

Romantic Beaches: Kefalonia is well-known for its beautiful beaches, many of which have a romantic feel to them. Some of the island's charming coastline treasures include the famed Myrtos Beach with its dramatic cliffs, Petani Beach with its hidden beauty, and Antisamos Beach with its crystal-clear seas. Couples may take a leisurely stroll down the beach, have a quiet picnic on the sand, or just relax and watch the sunset over the water.

Kefalonia's lovely villages, with their ancient architecture, small alleyways, and quaint tavernas, provide a romantic environment. Fiskardo, noted for its Venetian-style architecture, harborside cafés, and boutique stores, is a popular destination for couples. Assos offers a tranquil and beautiful environment, with pastel-colored cottages snuggled against a background of lush green hills. A romantic approach to spending time together is to stroll around these picturesque towns hand in hand.

Sunset Views: Kefalonia has breathtaking sunset views that add to the romantic ambience. Assos, positioned on a slope overlooking the sea, provides breathtaking views as the sun sets below the horizon. The Saint Theodoroi Lighthouse in Argostoli offers a great vantage point for watching the sunset. Couples may also enjoy the stunning hues of the sky at twilight by booking a sunset cruise or dining at a beach restaurant.

Kefalonia is well-known for its exceptional **wine production,** notably Robola wine. Couples may try a range of wines and learn about the island's winemaking traditions by visiting local wineries and vineyards, such as the Gentilini Winery. Sipping wine together in a romantic atmosphere surrounded by vineyards and stunning surroundings provides couples with a unique experience.

Private Boat Excursions: Take a private boat tour to explore the island's quiet coves, hidden beaches, and sea caves. Rent a boat or hire a captain for a private tour of the island's coastline. Discover hidden wonders like the Blue Caves or take a romantic day trip to nearby Ithaca. Enjoy the seclusion and tranquility of the sea while making memorable moments with your loved one.

Romantic Dining Experiences: Kefalonia has many romantic dining options for couples. Enjoy a romantic supper in a coastal taverna, where you may eat fresh fish and local specialties while listening to the waves. Some restaurants even have private dining choices on the beach or rooftop terraces, making for a more intimate environment for a romantic supper beneath the stars.

Spa Retreats: Indulge in a couples' spa getaway in Kefalonia. Several premium hotels and resorts on the island include spas where you and your partner may enjoy revitalizing treatments, massages, and wellness rituals. Relax and rest in a calm spa atmosphere, enabling the pressures of daily life to melt away and rekindle your relationship.

Hiking & Nature Walks: The varied landscapes of Kefalonia give chances for romantic treks and nature walks. Hand in hand, explore the paths of Mount Ainos National Park while taking in the natural beauty of the island. Discover secret waterfalls, picturesque vistas, and lush woods while relaxing in each other's company and taking in the scenery.

Kefalonia's rich history and culture provide couples with the opportunity to immerse themselves in real experiences. Learn about the importance of the Monastery of Saint Gerasimos, the island's patron saint. Discover ancient relics and exhibitions at Argostoli's Archaeological Museum. Attend local festivals and events to share your love of traditional music, dancing, and festivities.

Private Villa Retreats: Stay in a private villa in Kefalonia for the ideal romantic getaway. There are various villas for rent that provide solitude, luxury, and breathtaking views. Relax and spend quality time together in a peaceful and intimate location with your own pool, patio, and outdoor areas.

Photography Sessions: Capture your romantic moments in Kefalonia with a professional photograph. The natural beauty of the island provides a magnificent setting for your couple's photos. A skilled photographer can direct you to the most picturesque settings and capture your love in stunning shots.

Yoga and Meditation for Couples: Find inner calm and build your relationship with couples' yoga and meditation classes in Kefalonia. Many hotels and health resorts offer yoga classes or individual sessions in tranquil locations, enabling you to connect on a deeper level while also rejuvenating your mind and body.

Romantic Walks in Argostoli: Explore the picturesque capital city of Argostoli with your significant other. Take a walk down the waterfront promenade, taking in the views of the bay and browsing the local stores and boutiques. Visit ancient Lithostroto Street, which is dotted with cafés and restaurants where you may have a romantic lunch or a sweet treat.

Sunset Horseback Riding: Ride your horse across the scenery of Kefalonia. Many of the island's equestrian facilities offer guided horseback riding experiences, including sunset rides along the shore or into the countryside. Enjoy the serenity of nature as you ride together and take in the breathtaking hues of the sunset.

Cooking Lesson for Couples: Discover the delicacies of Kefalonia together with a cooking lesson for couples. Under the supervision of a qualified chef, learn to cook classic Greek delicacies such as moussaka or souvlaki. Enjoy the process of cooking together, and then relish the results as you eat together.

Romantic Cave Exploration: Go on a romantic journey by exploring the caverns on the island.

Melissani Cave, with its beautiful subterranean lake and lit chamber, provides a lovely environment for a boat trip with friends. Drogarati Cave, noted for its magnificent stalactites and stalagmites, offers a one-of-a-kind and awe-inspiring experience.

Wine and Olive Oil Tastings: Wine and olive oil tastings are a great way to learn about Kefalonia's culinary gems. Visit local vineyards and olive gardens to enjoy the best wines and olive oils on the island. Learn about the manufacturing processes and enjoy the fragrances and tastes of Kefalonian goods.

Private Helicopter Flight: A private helicopter flight above Kefalonia will take your romance to new heights. Aerial views of the island's spectacular coastline, rocky mountains, and attractive settlements are available. The spectacular views and the exhilaration of the helicopter trip will leave you with lasting memories.

Romantic Dinner Cruise: Take a romantic dinner cruise around Kefalonia's shoreline. Several organizations provide private boat trips with candlelight meals aboard, enabling you to enjoy a superb meal while surrounded by the tranquil beauty of the sea. Under the sky, savor delectable cuisine and toast to your love.

Relaxation on the Paliki Peninsula: Escape the throng and seek tranquility on the Paliki Peninsula, situated on Kefalonia's western coast. Explore quiet beaches like Xi and Vatsa where you can relax and enjoy each other's company in a tranquil and romantic atmosphere.

KEFALONIA FOR ADVENTURE SEEKERS

On this Greek island, adrenaline junkies will find lots of ways to satiate their desires. Kefalonia offers a variety of exhilarating excursions, from thrilling water sports to outdoor activities that display the island's natural beauty. For those looking for adventure, here are some information about Kefalonia:

Water Sports: The crystal-clear waters of Kefalonia are a great playground for water sports aficionados. Along the shore, try your hand at windsurfing, kiteboarding, or stand-up paddleboarding. Explore secret coves and isolated beaches by renting a kayak or a jet ski. Snorkeling and scuba diving are other popular sports for exploring the colorful underwater environment and marine life.

Hiking & Trekking: Put on your hiking boots and go out into the trails of Kefalonia. From seaside roads to mountain trails, the island provides a range of hiking routes that display its different scenery. Trek through Mount Ainos National Park to reach the peak and enjoy panoramic views of the island. Another gorgeous path that travels through vineyards and quaint towns, presenting a unique view of the island, is the Robola Wine Route.

Caving and Spelunking: Explore Kefalonia's subterranean treasures with caving and spelunking activities. The Drogarati Cave and the Melissani Cave are two of the island's intriguing caverns. Take guided trips down into these caves to marvel at spectacular stalactite and stalagmite formations and subterranean lakes.

Off-Road Activities: Off-road activities allow you to experience the rough beauty of Kefalonia's terrain. Join a jeep safari experience that takes you through gorgeous, off-the-beaten-path areas. Explore the natural delights of the island by traversing dirt roads, navigating steep slopes, and discovering secret overlooks. These tours often involve stops at secluded beaches and quaint villages, providing visitors with a unique viewpoint on Kefalonia.

Paragliding: Fly above the island and take in the gorgeous scenery with a paragliding adventure in Kefalonia. Take to the skies with a professional pilot and experience the thrill of flight. Admire the coastline, beaches, and mountains from above as you soar through the sky, making amazing memories.

Rock Climbing: Take on new challenges with rock climbing excursions in Kefalonia. Climbers of all ability levels may enjoy the island's cliffs and rock formations. Climbing routes with spectacular sea views are available, or you may opt to climb amid the lush foliage of the island's interior. Kefalonia provides an amazing opportunity to tackle the heights, whether you're a novice or an experienced climber.

Mountain biking allows you to explore the rocky terrain and gorgeous routes of Kefalonia on two wheels. Explore the island's landscape by mountain bike, riding through olive orchards, vineyards, and charming towns. Take on tough courses or enjoy leisurely rides while taking in the fresh air and magnificent scenery.

zoom-lining: Experience an adrenaline rush as you zoom through the trees on a zip-lining excursion. Several adventure parks in Kefalonia provide zip-line courses where you may fly from platform to platform while surrounded by the lovely trees of the island. Enjoy a thrilling ride and breathtaking sights from above.

Canyoning: Dive into the canyons of Kefalonia to experience the excitement of canyoning. Rappel down waterfalls, jump into natural pools, and descend through tiny valleys. These guided trips mix hiking, swimming, and rock climbing, offering a unique and thrilling approach to seeing the island's natural attractions.

Sailing & Yachting: Set off on a sailing or yachting expedition to experience the coastline of Kefalonia from the sea. Visit isolated beaches, secret caverns, and charming fishing towns by chartering a boat or joining a sailing excursion. Sail around the island, anchor in peaceful coves, and have a refreshing dip in crystal-clear waters. Enjoy the freedom and flexibility that comes with exploring the coast of Kefalonia by boat.

SHOPPING AND DINING

Shopping

Shopping in Kefalonia is a lovely mix of traditional items, local crafts, and one-of-a-kind souvenirs. The island has a wide range of shopping choices, from lively markets to lovely shops. Here's more information about shopping in Kefalonia:

Kefalonia is well-known for its superb **agricultural goods**, so shopping for local items is a necessity. Visit local markets or specialized stores to find a variety of treats such as olive oil, honey, wines, herbs, and traditional desserts. The rich soil and Mediterranean climate of the island contribute to the great quality and distinct flavors of these goods, making them ideal for culinary lovers or those seeking genuine sensations.

Kefalonia is home to brilliant artists who make wonderful **handcrafted goods**. Look for handwoven fabrics, delicate pottery, and hand-painted artwork that showcase the island's traditional artistry. Boutiques and art galleries in villages like Fiskardo and Assos display these one-of-a-kind masterpieces, enabling you to take a piece of Kefalonia's cultural legacy home with you.

Kefalonia is well-known for its **high-quality leather items,** particularly its handcrafted leather sandals. Explore the local shoemakers' workshops or boutique stores for elegant and comfy leather sandals made with care. Other leather accessories, including as belts, purses, and wallets, are also available, all produced with care and utilizing high-quality materials.

Fashion & Apparel: Kefalonia's principal towns, such as Argostoli and Lixouri, have a wide range of fashion shops and apparel stores. Explore the collections of Greek and worldwide designers to find fashionable apparel, beachwear, and accessories. From stylish resort apparel to contemporary beach gear, there are alternatives to suit all types and interests.

Kefalonia has a thriving jewelry culture, with local artists making stunning pieces inspired by the island's natural beauty. Look for handcrafted silver and gold jewelry with jewels, shells, or emblems of Kefalonia. These one-of-a-kind designs, ranging from delicate necklaces to elaborate bracelets, offer significant keepsakes or exceptional presents.

Antiques and Collectibles: Kefalonia is a treasure mine of antique stores and marketplaces for collectors. Discover antique furniture, collectibles, and one-of-a-kind objects that represent the history and cultural legacy of the island. Kefalonia's antique stores provide a fascinating shopping experience, whether you're a dedicated collector or just searching for a unique keepsake.

Souvenirs and Mementos: Bring a bit of Kefalonia home with you by purchasing souvenirs and mementos. Look for fridge magnets, postcards, and keychains with images of the island's renowned sights and emblems. Worry beads, evil eye charms, and olive wood goods are all traditional Greek handicrafts that make significant and symbolic mementos.

Food & Delicacies: Don't forget to shop for the famed Kefalonian delicacies. Discover a variety of goodies at the local delicatessens and food stores, such as local cheeses, cured meats, handmade preserves, and traditional pastries. These delicious treats not only make wonderful presents, but they also enable you to taste the flavors of Kefalonia long after your stay.

Bookshops: Bookworms and literary fans will enjoy the island's charming bookshops. Investigate the shelves stocked with Greek literature, area guidebooks, and works by local writers. Pick a book that embodies the spirit of Kefalonia's history, culture, or natural beauty and immerse yourself in the island's literary culture.

Markets & Bazaars: Visit Kefalonia's markets and bazaars to experience the colorful local atmosphere and get a flavor of daily life. These vibrant gatherings sell a variety of commodities such as fresh food, apparel, handicrafts, and household items. Engage with the locals, hone your negotiating abilities, and immerse yourself in the colorful atmosphere of these crowded marketplaces.

Explore Local Settlements: Go beyond the big cities and explore Kefalonia's smaller settlements. Shops and boutiques in Assos, Sami, and Lourdata provide a more genuine and personal shopping experience. You'll find local craftsmen and family-owned enterprises where you may locate hidden treasures and one-of-a-kind goods.

Visit Pottery Workshops: Kefalonia has a rich legacy of pottery manufacturing, which you can see by visiting the island's pottery workshops. View experienced artists at work and peruse their collections of plates, bowls, vases, and ornamental objects. Consider buying a piece of handcrafted pottery as a souvenir from your vacation.

Support Local Artists: Kefalonia has a vibrant creative community, and you can help by buying their work. Visit art galleries and exhibits to appreciate brilliant local artists' paintings, sculptures, and mixed-media works. Purchasing a work of art not only enables you to bring home a one-of-a-kind and meaningful keepsake, but it also helps to sustain the island's creative community.

Taste Local Wines: Kefalonia is well-known for its wine production, and a visit to the island is an excellent chance to tour local vineyards and try their wines. Visit vineyards or go on a wine tour to sample various varieties and learn about the winemaking process. If you discover wines you like, buy a bottle or two to enjoy later or to share with friends and family back home.

Natural Cosmetics: Kefalonia has a wide selection of natural and organic cosmetics created from local components. Look for boutiques or specialized stores that provide skincare, soaps, and other beauty products made with olive oil, honey, herbs, and other natural components. These items are delightful and nourishing mementos that encourage self-care and well-being.

While not a conventional shopping activity, sampling local foods is an integral part of the

Kefalonian experience. **Taste regional delicacies** including feta cheese, Kefalonian meat pie (Kreatopita), and Robola wine at local food markets and stores. These gourmet treats may be consumed at the moment or bought as delightful souvenirs of your journey.

Request Shopping Advice: Don't be afraid to ask locals or hotel personnel for shopping advice. They may give information on hidden treasures, local marketplaces, and establishments that sell real things. Engaging with locals and asking for their advice can enhance your shopping experience and help you uncover unusual discoveries that you would have missed otherwise.

Keep an Eye Out for Local Events: Find out if any local events, fairs, or festivals are taking place during your stay. These events often include local artists, craftspeople, and food producers, making them a fantastic chance to buy unique and locally crafted things straight from the source. These colorful events include traditional crafts, homemade items, and locally produced meals.

Bring Reusable Bags: Bring your own reusable bags to Kefalonia to be ecologically mindful when shopping. This reduces plastic waste and enables you to carry your items without using single-use plastic bags. Many Kefalonia establishments and marketplaces promote eco-friendly practices and urge customers to bring their own bags.

Check Customs Requirements: Before purchasing any mementos or items, educate yourself about your home country's customs requirements. Check for any limitations on transporting food, plants, or cultural objects back home. This will avoid any problems or delays while passing through customs.

When shopping in Kefalonia, don't forget to visit the smaller villages, where you'll discover delightful shops and local artists displaying their wares. Look for locally manufactured handicrafts and one-of-a-kind souvenirs that genuinely represent the island's uniqueness and charm.

Dining

Kefalonia dining is a pleasant experience that mixes classic Greek cuisines with the island's own distinct culinary influences. Kefalonia has a broad choice of eating alternatives to meet every appetite, from fresh fish to local specialties. Here's a look at where to eat in Kefalonia:

Kefalonia is well-known for its delectable Greek food, which offers fresh, high-quality ingredients and simple but savory meals. Moussaka (layers of eggplant, minced beef, and béchamel sauce), souvlaki (grilled skewered meat), and spanakopita (spinach pie) are all traditional Greek foods. Try kreatopita (meat pie), sofrito (veal cooked in a white wine and garlic sauce), and bourdeto (spicy fish stew) as local favorites.

Fresh Fish: Kefalonia, being an island, has an abundance of fresh fish. Visit seaside towns and fishing villages to sample the day's catch. Try grilled octopus, fried calamari, or fresh fish with olive oil, lemon, and herbs. Local taverns and seafood restaurants provide a broad variety of seafood meals, enabling you to experience the tastes of the Mediterranean.

Local Products: The rich land and Mediterranean environment of Kefalonia aid in the development of high-quality local products. Take advantage of the fresh fruits, veggies, and herbs available on the island. Juicy tomatoes, crisp cucumbers, fragrant herbs like oregano and thyme, and savory olives are also on the menu. Salads, side dishes, and traditional meals often use these items.

Kefalonia is well-known for its outstanding olive oil. The island's olive fields provide some of Greece's best extra virgin olive oil. Drizzle this golden elixir over salads, or grilled meats, or serve as a dip with freshly baked bread. You may even go to a local olive oil producer to learn about the production process and buy some to take home.

Wineries and Vineyards: Kefalonia has a strong winemaking heritage, and the vineyards on the island produce superb wines. Explore the nearby vineyards and sample the famed Robola wine, a crisp white wine created from the Kefalonian grape variety Robola. Discover the island's rich wine culture by visiting vineyards, learning about the winemaking process, and partaking in wine tastings.

Traditional Greek Meze: Celebrate the Greek custom of meze by ordering a selection of small meals to enjoy with friends and family. Tzatziki (yogurt and cucumber dip), dolmades (stuffed grape leaves), feta cheese, and grilled halloumi are among the appetizers available. Meze is an excellent opportunity to sample a variety of cuisines while also enjoying a sociable meal experience.

Local Bakeries: Kefalonia's bakeries provide a delectable selection of freshly baked delicacies. Begin your day with a traditional Greek breakfast of freshly made bread and pastries, followed by a strong cup of Greek coffee. As a tasty snack, try the renowned Kefalonian meat pie (kreatopita) or cheese pie (tiropita). Sweet delights such as baklava, loukoumades (honey-soaked doughnuts), or indigenous Kefalonian sweets such as mandolato (nougat) or pasteli (sesame seed and honey bars) should not be missed.

Waterside Dining: Many restaurants in Kefalonia have wonderful waterside locations, allowing you to dine while admiring the sea. Choose a restaurant near the shore, such as Fiskardo, Lassi, or Argostoli, and appreciate your lunch while taking in the quiet environment and breathtaking views. It's a once-in-a-lifetime eating experience.

Farm-to-Table Experiences: Consider engaging in a farm-to-table experience to have a better understanding of the island's cuisine. Some local farms and agritourism businesses provide tours and dining experiences where you may learn about traditional agricultural techniques, gather fresh produce, and enjoy a meal made with locally sourced ingredients. It's a chance to get in touch with the land and the tastes of Kefalonia.

Greek Sweets: Traditional Greek sweets will round off your dining experience in Kefalonia. Baklava (layers of filo pastry, almonds, and honey syrup), galaktoboureko (custard-filled pastry), and loukoumades (fried dough balls coated with honey and dusted with cinnamon) are all delicious. These sweet delights round out your dinner and give you a sense of the island's gastronomic history.

Keep in mind that Greeks prefer leisurely meals, so take your time, appreciate each mouthful, and embrace the easygoing eating atmosphere while dining in Kefalonia. Also, don't be afraid to ask locals or restaurant employees for ideas, as they may give insight into the greatest cuisine and eating venues on the island.

Some Dishes You Should Try When You Visit Kefalonia

When visiting Kefalonia, you'll have the opportunity to indulge in a variety of delicious dishes that showcase the island's rich culinary heritage. Here are ten must-try dishes that represent the flavors and traditions of Kefalonia:

Kreatopita: Kreatopita is a traditional Kefalonian meat pie that is a true delight for meat lovers. It consists of layers of tender meat, often beef or veal, cooked with onions, garlic, and herbs, sandwiched between layers of flaky pastry. The result is a hearty and flavorful pie that is perfect for a satisfying lunch or dinner.

Bourdeto: This spicy fish stew is a staple in Kefalonian cuisine. It typically features fish like scorpionfish or cod cooked in a rich tomato sauce with garlic, onions, and hot red pepper flakes. The combination of flavors creates a zesty and aromatic dish that pairs well with crusty bread or a side of potatoes.

Sofrito: Sofrito is a signature dish of Kefalonia, made with thinly sliced veal cooked in a white wine and garlic sauce. The meat is slowly simmered until tender, resulting in a melt-in-your-mouth texture. The flavors are enhanced by the addition of bay leaves and a squeeze of lemon juice, creating a delightful balance of savory and tangy notes.

Robola Salad: Robola salad is a refreshing and light dish that showcases the island's famous Robola wine.

It combines fresh greens, cherry tomatoes, cucumbers, red onions, and feta cheese, drizzled with a dressing made from olive oil, lemon juice, and a splash of Robola wine. It's a perfect choice for a light lunch or a side dish to accompany your main course.

Ladopita: Ladopita is a unique and decadent dessert that Kefalonia is known for. It consists of thin layers of dough brushed with olive oil, sprinkled with cinnamon and sugar, and baked to a golden crisp. The result is a crispy, flaky treat that is often served warm and dusted with powdered sugar. It's a delightful way to end a meal.

Savoro: Savoro is a traditional Greek dish that is particularly popular in Kefalonia. It features small fish, typically fried or grilled, and then marinated in a mixture of vinegar, white wine, garlic, and herbs. The marinade infuses the fish with a tangy and aromatic flavor, making it a delicious appetizer or main course.

Petimezi: Petimezi is a traditional sweet syrup made from grape must. It's used as a natural sweetener in various dishes and desserts in Kefalonia. Drizzle it over yogurt or use it as a topping for pancakes or ice cream. Its deep, rich flavor adds a touch of sweetness to any dish.

Rabbit Stifado: Rabbit stifado is a hearty and flavorful stew made with rabbit meat, onions, garlic, red wine, and a blend of aromatic spices. The slow cooking process allows the flavors to meld together, resulting in tender meat and a rich, savory sauce. It's a popular dish in Kefalonia, especially during festive occasions.

Avgolemono Soup: Avgolemono soup is a comforting and nourishing Greek soup made with chicken broth, lemon juice, and eggs. It's thickened to a creamy consistency and often served with orzo pasta. The combination of tangy lemon and rich chicken broth creates a satisfying and comforting flavor profile.

Baklava: Baklava is a beloved Greek dessert that is also popular in Kefalonia. It consists of layers of flaky filo pastry filled with a mixture of chopped nuts, such as walnuts or almonds, and sweetened with a syrup made from honey, lemon juice, and cinnamon. It's a sweet and indulgent treat that pairs well with a cup of Greek coffee or a scoop of vanilla ice cream.

NIGHTLIFE IN KEFALONIA

Here are some information concerning Kefalonia's nightlife:

Beach Bars: During the summer, several of Kefalonia's major beaches feature beach bars that come alive. These pubs provide a relaxed ambiance where you may have a refreshing drink or a cool beer while gazing out at the sea. Special events, such as live music performances or beach parties, are often held in beach bars, creating a vibrant and fun atmosphere.

Cocktail Bars: There are various cocktail bars in Kefalonia where you may sip perfectly created beverages in a fashionable and sophisticated atmosphere. These establishments often provide a broad range of inventive cocktails made with fresh local ingredients and quality alcohol. Relax in a comfortable lounge or on the open-air patio while sipping your favorite beverage.

Tavernas and Restaurants: In addition to wonderful cuisine, many of Kefalonia's tavernas and restaurants provide nightly entertainment. You may have a leisurely supper while listening to live music, which may include traditional Greek music or current covers. These establishments provide a pleasant and genuine atmosphere in which to enjoy a meal while immersing yourself in the island's culture.

Music Bars and Clubs: Kefalonia features music bars and clubs that appeal to night owls for those looking for a livelier ambiance. You may spend the night dancing to a range of music genres, such as Greek music, worldwide hits, and electronic rhythms. Some establishments feature guest DJs and themed events, guaranteeing a lively and thrilling nightlife experience.

Kefalonia boasts **open-air theatres** that provide a unique and dramatic way to see a movie beneath the sky. These theatres usually show both Greek and foreign films, and you can have a snack or a drink from the concession stand as you sit back and relax in a calm outdoor atmosphere.

Kefalonia has a variety of cultural events during the summer, including music festivals, theatrical performances, and art exhibits. These activities take place in a variety of locations around the island, including historic landmarks, outdoor stages, and cultural institutions. Attending these events allows you to immerse yourself in the local art scene and discover the island's cultural diversity.

Nighttime Excursions: The natural beauty of Kefalonia continues into the night, and you may take nighttime excursions to see the island's distinctive landscapes after dark. You may, for example, join a guided boat excursion to experience the captivating bioluminescence in the sea, where the water lights with phosphorescent light. This delightful encounter is genuinely wonderful, providing a new perspective on Kefalonia's natural beauty.

Kefalonia features a **casino** where you may try your luck at several games of chance if you're feeling fortunate. Slot machines, blackjack, roulette, and poker are among the games available at the casino. It's a fantastic spot to try your luck and spend an exciting evening of entertainment.

Sunset Cruises: Kefalonia's stunning sunsets are a sight to see, and you may enhance the experience by going on a sunset cruise. These excursions usually leave from the port and carry you along the coast, where you can see the beautiful hues of the sky as the sun sets over the Ionian Sea. Some cruises feature live music, supper, and beverages, making for a wonderful and romantic evening.

Joining a pub crawl or arranging your own bar-hopping tour may be a great way to enjoy Kefalonia's nightlife if you want to explore the local bar scene and meet other visitors. You may visit several bars and pubs, try various beverages, and enjoy the bustling environment as you go from one location to another.

It's important to note that the nightlife in Kefalonia changes based on the season and location. The summer months, particularly July and August, are the most colorful and busiest with nightlife alternatives on the island. Even during the shoulder seasons, though, you may find restaurants operating and giving entertainment. To make the most of your night out in Kefalonia, always check the local listings and ask for suggestions.

ACCOMMODATION OPTIONS IN KEFALONIA

Kefalonia has a variety of lodging alternatives to meet any traveler's interests and budget. The island offers a wide range of accommodations, from luxury resorts and boutique hotels to quaint guesthouses and self-catering flats, for a pleasant and unforgettable visit. Here is a rundown of the lodging alternatives in Kefalonia:

Kefalonia is home to various **luxury resorts** that provide unrivaled comfort and services. These resorts often include large rooms or suites with excellent furniture, private balconies or terraces, and breathtaking views of the sea or surrounding countryside. Swimming pools, spa and wellness centers, exercise centers, gourmet restaurants, and exclusive beach access are examples of on-site amenities. The resorts are often placed in scenic locations, enabling visitors to relax and enjoy a sumptuous island break.

Kefalonia has a number of beautiful **boutique hotels** that blend individual service with distinctive design and ambience. These smaller-scale lodgings sometimes include attractively appointed rooms or suites with contemporary facilities. The pleasant and welcoming ambience is created by the tiny setting, and the staff is noted for their attention to detail and genuine hospitality. Boutique hotels in Kefalonia are often located in great locations, such as along the seaside or inside ancient towns, and provide a unique combination of convenience and charm.

Traditional Guesthouses: Consider staying in a traditional guesthouse or a family-run pension for a more genuine and personal experience. These lodgings are often situated in ancient towns or rural settings, enabling you to immerse yourself in local culture and experience the island's traditional way of life. The proprietors are recognized for their warm hospitality and particular care, and the guesthouses often provide snug and comfortable rooms with modest furniture. You may have handmade breakfasts cooked with local ingredients and frequently get insider suggestions on the finest places to see and eat in the region.

Self-Catering Apartments and Villas: Self-catering apartments and villas are a popular alternative in Kefalonia if you desire more flexibility and freedom during your visit. These hotels provide fully equipped kitchens or kitchenettes, enabling you to cook your own meals and dine at your leisure. Apartments vary from small studios to enormous multi-room homes, whilst villas sometimes have private swimming pools and outside areas, making them perfect for families or larger parties. These self-catering alternatives are accessible around the island, including coastal villas and tranquil rural getaways.

Beachfront Hotels: Kefalonia is known for its beautiful beaches, and staying in one enables you to take advantage of the island's natural beauty. These hotels have immediate beach access, enabling you to wake up to the sound of the waves and spend your days relaxing on the sand. The rooms or suites are often sea-facing, assuring stunning views, and may include amenities such as beach loungers, umbrellas, and seaside cafés or restaurants.

Agrotourism & Rural Retreats: Consider vacationing in an agrotourism institution or a rural retreat for a unique and immersive experience. These lodgings are usually found in the countryside, surrounded by vineyards, olive trees, or farmland. They give a peaceful respite from the busy coastal regions and a chance to reconnect with nature. Guests may engage in agricultural activities such as olive or grape picking or just rest in the tranquil surroundings. The accommodations vary from old farmhouses that have been refurbished to contemporary eco-friendly cottages that combine rustic beauty with modern amenities.

Camping and Caravan Sites: For those who want a more adventurous and outdoorsy experience, Kefalonia boasts various camping and caravan sites. These facilities include dedicated spots for tents, campervans, and caravans, as well as amenities such as shared cooking areas, barbeque areas, and restrooms. Camping enables you to get closer to nature and explore the island at your own speed.

Agia Efimia: This little beach hamlet has a variety of lodging alternatives, including modest hotels and flats. Staying at Agia Efimia puts you near magnificent beaches, boat rentals for exploring the coast, and a variety of waterfront tavernas offering fresh seafood.

Lixouri: Located on the Paliki Peninsula, Lixouri is a bustling town with a range of lodging options. Hotels, guesthouses, and self-catering flats may be found here. The streets of Lixouri are lined with traditional tavernas, cafés, and businesses, creating a bustling environment.

Skala: Skala is a prominent Kefalonia tourist attraction noted for its long sandy beach and active nightlife. The town has a variety of lodging options, including hotels and flats. Staying in Skala gives you convenient access to beach activities, water sports, and a vibrant town center filled with restaurants and bars.

Sami is a seaside village on Kefalonia's east coast famed for its scenic port and closeness to major sites such as Melissani Cave. Sami has a variety of hotels and residences, and its central position makes it an ideal starting point for touring the island.

Assos: Assos is a lovely hamlet located in a gorgeous harbor, crowned by a Venetian castle. Small hotels and flats are available for accommodation in Assos. Staying in Assos provides a peaceful environment, breathtaking views, and the chance to visit the castle remains and adjacent beaches.

Agia Pelagia: Located on Kefalonia's southern coast, Agia Pelagia is a little fishing hamlet famed for its crystal-clear seas and quiet atmosphere. Small hotels, flats, and studios are available in Agia Pelagia. It's an excellent choice for people looking for a peaceful and relaxed break.

Poros: Poros is a seaside town on Kefalonia's southeast coast with a lovely port and a sandy beach. Hotels and apartments with sea views are available for rent in Poros. The community has a relaxed vibe, waterfront tavernas, and convenient access to boat tours to adjacent islands.

Katelios is a quiet fishing community on the island's southern coast famed for its sandy beaches and traditional tavernas. In Katelios, you may stay in family-run guesthouses or apartments. It's an excellent option for people looking for a tranquil and genuine Greek experience.

When reserving accommodation in Kefalonia, keep in mind aspects like accessibility to attractions, facilities provided, and the sort of experience you want. Also, consider the time of year you want to travel, since certain sites and lodgings may be restricted during the high season.

BEST TRAVEL RESOURCES

These are the best travel resources I usually use:

SkyScanner: This is my favorite flight search engine of all time. It always appears to discover the greatest rates, and its calendar display shows you when days are the most affordable to travel. It appeals to me since it searches little booking sites that no one else does. Begin all of your flight searches here.

Momodo: This fantastic website searches a wide range of airlines, including several low-cost carriers that bigger sites overlook. While I usually start with Skyscanner, I'll also look at this site to compare costs.

Google Flights: Google Flights allows you to input your departure airport and view flights all around the globe on a map to get the cheapest destination. It's a useful search engine for learning about routes, connections, and prices.

Hostelworld: The market's most user-friendly hostel website, with the greatest inventory, the finest search interface, and the most availability. You may also look for private rooms or dorm beds. I use it for my reservations.

Couchsurfing: This website enables you to stay for free on people's sofas or in their spare rooms. It's a terrific way to save money while meeting locals who can teach you a lot more about a place than a hostel or hotel can. There are also groups on the web where you can organize to meet up for activities in your location.

Booking.com: Booking.com is an excellent resource for low-cost hotels and other forms of lodging. I enjoy how simple its UI is.

Trusted Housesitters: Try house- or pet-sitting for a novel (and free) way to travel. You just care after someone's home and/or pet while they are gone in return for free lodging. It's an excellent choice for long-term travelers and those on a tight budget.

CONCLUSION

In conclusion, Kefalonia is a captivating destination that offers a myriad of experiences for travelers seeking natural beauty, cultural richness, and a relaxed island atmosphere. From its stunning beaches and picturesque villages to its historical sites and delicious cuisine, Kefalonia has something to enchant every visitor.

The island's diverse landscapes provide ample opportunities for outdoor activities and exploration. Whether you're hiking through the lush Mount Ainos National Park, diving into the crystal-clear waters, or cruising along the coastline, you'll be immersed in Kefalonia's breathtaking beauty. Don't miss the chance to visit iconic attractions like Myrtos Beach, Melissani Cave, Assos Village, and the Lighthouse of Saint Theodoroi.

Kefalonia's cultural festivals and holidays offer a glimpse into the island's traditions and celebrations. Witnessing the vibrant processions of the Saint Gerasimos Festival or experiencing the joyful atmosphere of the Carnival will leave you with lasting memories of Kefalonia's cultural heritage.

When it comes to accommodation, Kefalonia caters to a wide range of preferences and budgets. Whether you choose a luxury resort, a charming boutique hotel, a traditional guesthouse, or a self-catering apartment, you'll find comfortable and welcoming options throughout the island. Each type of accommodation provides its own unique charm and allows you to immerse yourself in the island's hospitality.

Kefalonia's culinary scene is a delight for food lovers, with its fresh and flavorful dishes. Don't miss the opportunity to savor local specialties such as Robola wine, Kefalonian meat pie, fresh seafood, and the famous Kefalonian honey. Dining in Kefalonia is a celebration of the island's bountiful produce and traditional recipes.

The island also offers a vibrant nightlife, with beach bars, cocktail lounges, music venues, and open-air cinemas. Whether you prefer a relaxed evening by the sea or a lively night out on the town, Kefalonia's nightlife scene will not disappoint.

As you explore Kefalonia, take advantage of the numerous day trips available to nearby islands and attractions. From the picturesque island of Ithaca to the fascinating ancient ruins of Olympia on the mainland, these excursions offer additional opportunities to discover the wonders of the region.

Whether you're traveling as a family, a couple, or an adventure seeker, Kefalonia offers an abundance of activities and experiences that cater to every traveler's desires. With its natural beauty, rich history, warm hospitality, and delectable cuisine, Kefalonia promises a truly memorable vacation.

As you plan your trip to Kefalonia, consider the best time to visit, taking into account the weather, crowd levels, and specific events or festivals you may want to experience. Research and book accommodations and activities in advance to ensure a smooth and enjoyable trip.

In Kefalonia, you'll discover an island that combines stunning landscapes, rich culture, and warm hospitality, creating an unforgettable destination that will leave you longing to return. So pack your bags, immerse yourself in the magic of Kefalonia, and create memories that will last a lifetime.

Printed in Great Britain
by Amazon

27881589R00112